"*Take two minutes in the morning and read any chapter. You will find something that makes you a better parent and helps you enjoy your family more that day.*"

—Melvin V. Gerbie, M.D.,
Chief, Section of Gynecology,
Northwestern University Medical School

"*Wonderful stories and ideas to help families connect or re-connect . . . An excellent resource.*"

—Kenneth Polin, M.D., Pediatrician

"*How delightful! Allows parents to understand the gift that they are receiving. There are so many helpful tips on parenting and just living.*"

—Beth Ylvisaker, Artist and Mother

Also by Susan Smith Kuczmarski
Values-Based Leadership (with Tom Kuczmarski)

Praise for *The Family Bond*

"*Simple, easily replicated activities guide the reader to an understanding of the importance of connections in creating strong families. The Family Bond is an absolute must-read.*"

—Galeta Kaar Clayton,
Founding Headmistress,
Chicago Day School

"*An eloquent, funny, deceptively easy-to-read and important-to-think-about guide to creating an atmosphere in which dynamic and active love can thrive.*"

—Terry Spencer Hesser,
Television Producer and
Author, *Kissing Doorknobs*

"*My left brain told me that the exercises in* The Family Bond *appear highly effective. My better half, my right brain, and my father heart, experienced the enormous creativity of this approach to parenting.*"

—John R. Cooper, Ph.D.,
Clinical Psychologist and
President, Impact Consultants

"This book reminds us of the importance of understanding our children's point of view and offers us simple ideas on how to be open to the joys of everyday life while creating rituals that will become lasting memories for our families."

—Jane Nolan, Teacher,
Park West Cooperative Nursery School

"A fresh way of addressing the issues of parenting. Rather than approaching the topic from the point of discipline, the author has begun with the concept of building love and respect from within the family."

—Catherine F. Beadles, Teacher

"A delight to read and recommend. 'Familyweaving' is a concept that can help even the most time-starved mother or father. The author's ideas for bringing families together are truly inspiring."

—Colleen Dudgeon-Ransdell,
Television Producer

The Family Bond

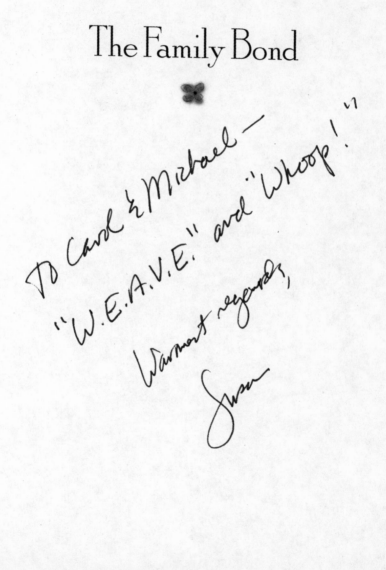

To Carol & Michael —
"W.E.A.V.E." and "Whoop!"

Warmest regards,

Susan

The Family Bond

Inspiring Tips for Creating a Closer Family

SUSAN SMITH KUCZMARSKI, ED.D.

CONTEMPORARY BOOKS

Library of Congress Cataloging-in-Publication Data

Kuczmarski, Susan Smith.
    The family bond : inspiring tips for creating a closer family /
Susan Smith Kuczmarski.
        p.   cm.
     ISBN 0-8092-2391-0
     1. Family.   I. Title.
  HQ518.K83   2000
  306.85—dc21
                                     99-44711
                                       CIP

Cover design by Mary Lockwood
Interior design by Susan H. Hartman
Interior illustrations by Robert Wilmott

Published by Contemporary Books
A division of NTC/Contemporary Publishing Group, Inc.
4255 West Touhy Avenue, Lincolnwood (Chicago), Illinois 60712-1975 U.S.A.
Printed in the United States of America
International Standard Book Number: 0-8092-2391-0

00 01 02 03 04 05 LB 18 17 16 15 14 13 12 11 10 9 8 7 6 5 4 3 2 1

To Thomas D. Kuczmarski,
partner, innovator, and educator,
and to our sons, John, James, and Thomas,
teachers and friends forever

Contents

Acknowledgments

I am enormously grateful to my husband, Tom, my best friend and partner in life and familymaking, who lent his wisdom, encouragement, and support at every phase of this project; to my special friend, Martha Donovan, our "Aunt Muppie," who taught me how to write more gracefully through her own inner beauty, and who has been a part of our own family's journey; to Kim Grant, who edited each draft with her internal fortitude and fine-tuned skills; to Susan Shapiro, who formatted the completed manuscript with her creative, intuitive hands; to Robert Wilmott, who produced the drawings with humor and artistry; to the entire publishing team at NTC/Contemporary Books, especially to Judith McCarthy for her vision and professionalism, Kristen Eberhard for her guidance in the production process, Kimberly Soenen for her extraordinary expertise and generous spirit, and Danielle Egan-Miller for opening the door; and finally, to my own parents, Fernando and Bula Smith, our "Papa" and "Beah," who taught me how to laugh and give.

Introduction

Children are our gold and families are our most valuable cultural resource. Yet we are not trained for the job of familymaking. No course is offered that teaches us how to bring families closer together. Nor are we born with this information. And much of what we learned from our own parents, given our constantly changing world, cannot be reapplied. While my training as a cultural anthropologist has taught me to look for patterns, I wrote this book because I have a passion for parenting. My own search for the ways to become a better parent led to many insights about what makes family life more difficult and what makes it easier. I offer this book as a way of sharing my learning.

A good teacher does much more than lecture. This teacher arranges learning situations to help each student find his or her own inner voice. Parenting is about teaching too, and about helping your child find her own inner voice. Too much "parent talk" can actually get in the way. So can excessive "teacher talk." (Chapters are short for this reason, with most of them three to four pages long. Some are even less; only a few are more; and each chapter ends with a "learning nugget" that summarizes what I want to share with you.)

I hope this book helps you learn to teach in a way that helps your child find her inner voice—and helps you hear yours more clearly as well.

The Family Bond

PART I

Clear Seeing

Ordinary Magic

*"'When you wake up in the morning, Pooh,' said Piglet,
'What's the first thing you say to yourself?'*

*'What's for breakfast,' said Pooh. 'What do you say,
Piglet?'*

*'I say, I wonder what's going to happen exciting
today,' replied Piglet.*

Pooh nodded thoughtfully, 'It's the same thing,' he said."

—A. A. Milne, *Winnie-the-Pooh*

It's true. The simple, ordinary things have extraordinary magic. For Pooh, it's breakfast. For Piglet, it's the unfolding of the events of the day. He believes they will be exciting and can't wait for them to begin. Family life is a series of events that offers this same extraordinary magic. Total involvement in daily life presents a formula for happiness. Very simply, in experiencing the ordinary events of the day (whether it's just eating breakfast like Pooh or letting the day unfold like Piglet), there is extraordinary magic because each event can serve as a pathway to growth and discovery.

One Christmas morning, when my son James was eight years old, he lay awake while his two brothers slept. He was unusually quiet, especially given the excitement that was soon to unfold. When I asked him what he was doing to keep so occupied, he said he was planning Jesus's birthday party. He had already decided what games he was going to play at the party. They were three games that we often play at our own children's birthday celebrations: pin-the-tail-on-the-donkey, hide and go seek, and the hat game—a variation of musical chairs.

There is a natural magic to children. If I hadn't asked him what he was thinking that morning, I would have missed it. Pooh and Piglet each looked forward to different things, but they still connected through the magic of ordinary events. Our families can do that too.

PARENTING MEANS SHARING AND
APPRECIATING THE EXTRAORDINARY MAGIC
OF ORDINARY DAILY EVENTS.

2

Using Both Sides
of the Brain

The brain has two halves, each with a different style of thinking and a different energy. Henriette Klauser clarifies the role of each side in her helpful book *Writing on Both Sides of the Brain* (San Francisco: HarperSanFrancisco, 1987). The left brain is the know-it-all. It is the master of expressing itself logically, verbally, and in written words. It is analytical, rational, objective, and detail oriented as it focuses on each step in any process. The right side is sometimes called "the silent partner"; it expresses itself randomly, through rhythms, patterns, and pictures. It cannot articulate itself in words. It is visual, intuitive, subjective, and overview oriented as it focuses on the interrelationships between the steps in any process. The left side is time centered and the right side is timeless. The left side is linguistic, while the right is musical. The left side is aggressive, while the right side is yielding.

Betty Edwards, in her book *Drawing on the Right Side of the Brain* (Los Angeles: J. P. Tarcher, 1979), shows us the power of using both sides of the brain. She believes that everyone can draw, even those who don't think they can. First, she asks her students to draw a picture of Picasso's "Portrait of Igor Stravinsky." Then she asks them to turn the Picasso portrait upside down and draw it again. When the students compare the two drawings, they find that the right-side-up one is quite poor, while the upside-down one is rather good. Edwards offers the

following explanation: "The left brain refused the task of processing the upside-down image. Presumably, the left hemisphere, confused and blocked by the unfamiliar image, turned off, and the job passed over to the right hemisphere." The left brain is forced to admit that the right brain did a better job.

Parenting, at least within our Western society, has ignored this "right-brained" way of thinking. Take a look at all the how-to books available to parents. Most of them focus on the left-brain aspect of parenting, or how to evaluate and change behaviors. But parenting is a whole-brain activity. The energy of the left side says "take charge," while the energy of the right side says "flow." If we learn to balance the left side with the right side, what might happen to our families? I believe we can learn to use both sides of the brain and "draw" families that think and express emotion openly, freely, and heartfully.

USE YOUR *WHOLE BRAIN* TO DRAW YOUR
FAMILY TOGETHER.

3

Inside the Boa Constrictor

"My drawing was not a picture of a hat. It was a picture of a boa constrictor digesting an elephant. But since the grown-ups were not able to understand it, I made another drawing: I drew the inside of the boa constrictor so that the grown-ups could see it clearly. They always need to have things explained."

—Antoine de Saint-Exupéry, *The Little Prince*

Values, like drawings, are highly personal choices. Children have their own values, and it is very important to let them surface. Seeing clearly what you value is the first step. Write down your values, and have your child write his values down too. If your child is quite young, write them down for him.

Let me share with you my family's values, which we had great fun writing down one warm summer night: My fifteen-year-old John values time to relax, think, read, and play; he likes to be in control, express his feelings, and be assertive; he values honesty, loyalty, humor, "total play," flexibility, knowledge, supportiveness, uniqueness, and self-esteem. My thirteen-year-old James values having fun, playing with friends, spending time with each family member, doing "crazy things," going on fun excursions during the school day, and pursuing hobbies. My eight-year-old Thomas values kindness, helpfulness, and time to play and read books. My husband values consideration and respect for others, belief in diversity, respect of self, loyalty, thoughtfulness, kindness, achievement, and love. I value a sense of humor, laughter, the beauty of differences, ongoing growth and learning, family, time, and a spiritual relationship.

After you identify and list your individual values, take a very close look at them. Prioritize your top five values and write them down. Have each member of your family do the

same. Next, have each person talk about his or her values while the entire family listens deeply. Then, have your family decide together which values they should all adopt as the "family values." This doesn't mean that the individual abandons those personal values not selected by the group. Those values will always be important to that person, but the family needs to have its own set of values. (It is important, however, that a family's values include at least some of the values of each individual member.)

Simply put, identifying values—individual and family—takes the following steps:

Stage I: Individual Values Development
1. List your own personal values.
2. Prioritize your top five values (this is hard; keep them all if you want).
3. "Publish" a list of each individual's values for the family to discuss.

Stage II: Family Values Development
1. Review individual values and identify the group's top choices.
2. Develop a set of group values.
3. Design specific ways to activate and reinforce these values and make them part of your lives.

When we put our individual values together, this is what we came up with as our family values:

Our Family's Shared Values
+ Recognize time as a gift.
+ Play, read, think, relax, and have fun, crazy times together.
+ Laugh often and cultivate a sense of humor.
+ Build self-esteem in each other.
+ Be assertive, express feelings, and exercise control over one's own life.
+ See diversity as a strength. Each person is unique, interesting, and different.
+ Recognize the beauty of loyalty, friendship, and love.
+ Express consideration and respect for others; be thoughtful, kind, helpful, supportive, and flexible.
+ Seek to always learn and grow; pursue knowledge, hobbies, personal achievement, and spiritual understanding.

If children aren't allowed or encouraged to identify their own values now, they will confront years of doubt in the future. Over time, rather than saying "these things are important to me," children will have difficulty identifying what matters in their lives. What is deeply important to them will become increasingly unclear. They won't see the boa constrictor digesting an elephant anymore—just the hat! They won't want to talk anymore about "boa constrictors, or primeval forests, or stars," and eventually they too will become grown-ups who don't understand. The life-shaping decisions of what is important will be made by other people who impose their own ideas and values onto them.

If children are aware of their values from an early age, they will know what is significant to them. Then, within the groups in which they live—whether classroom, friends, or future work settings—they will be able to recognize what interests outweigh others. When children have been encouraged to know what they value, they will be able to have greater involvement in, and control over, their life choices.

❈

IN DESCRIBING THEIR VALUES, FAMILIES CAN
HELP THEIR MEMBERS SEE WHAT MATTERS
MOST IN THEIR LIVES.

4

Working by Looking

A young apprentice was observing how his master looked at each object he was planning to paint. It appeared as though the master painter sat staring at the objects for long periods of time. Whether a pot, a person, or a drape, he stared deeply at it. When asked why he looked so intensely at these pieces, the master replied, "I am working, working by looking." This was difficult for the young apprentice to understand. But as time passed, he too learned to sit and look at each object until it was "in his fingers" before he began to paint it.

The master's stare analyzed the colors. The piece of material on the chair might appear to be blue, but there is violet in the blue and a faint touch of rose. Even red and green can be found in the highlights. "Look again," he tells the apprentice.

Suddenly, he too could see the other colors. "The eye is complicated. It mixes the colors for you," said the master. "The painter must unmix them and lay them on again shade by shade. Then the eye of the beholder takes over and mixes them again." This is a story of Juan de Pareja, who was an apprentice to the great master painter Diego Velázquez in seventeenth-century Spain, as told by Elizabeth Borton de Trevino in *I, Juan de Pareja* (New York: Farrar, Straus & Giroux, 1965).

The apprentice painter must learn to look, then look again. He must look until he can feel the shape of the lines and

colors in his fingers before he can paint. As parents, we too must learn to look, then look again. Children have lines and colors too, and these are their strengths and needs. Parenting means working by looking. It means learning the child's colors and being able to unmix them to see their strengths and needs.

As parents, we must look closely to see these strengths and needs in our children, then help them to see their unique colors for themselves. If a child is aware of her colors, she knows that her heart has been felt and her strengths have been seen. This knowledge can become a powerful brush to create a magical and elegant life.

❧

FIND YOUR CHILD'S "TRUE COLORS" BY
DETERMINING HER STRENGTHS AND NEEDS.

5

Unmixing Colors—
Becoming Visible

Picture an artist's palette with globs of different colored paints lined up in a curve around the hole where the painter holds onto it. Each color on the palette becomes one of the artist's choices. With brush in hand, the artist is ready to mix the paints together and apply them to the canvas. But before the artist begins, let's look closely at the individual colors.

Parents, do you know your colors? Do you know what makes you visible? You must learn your own strengths and needs before you can help your children learn theirs. Work by looking—like the artist. What are your specific strengths and needs? List three of each now.

Just like a beautiful painting emerges from the mix of colors, a vibrant family is born out of careful attention to the shades and hues of each of its members. In a strong family, children and parents alike will show their strengths and express their needs. They will grow and develop individually and nourish one another. Help your children become visible. Teach them how to see their own separate colors. What strengths and needs do they have? What colors make them unique?

Have each family member do his or her own list of strengths and needs, share them, and get some input from other family members. Knowing who I am and what my needs are and who you are and what your needs are can help us choose activities for personal growth and fun. What do you want to learn, acquire, and achieve? How can you find ways to satisfy your personal needs? What can parents do to facilitate this personal growth? And what can siblings do to help one another? Family members can help each individual find the right path to personal growth by matching every strength and need with at least one activity or action. These can be developed into individual growth goals and plans for each family member.

IDENTIFY EACH FAMILY MEMBER'S STRENGTHS SO THAT EACH PERSON CAN DEVELOP THEIR GOALS AND VISIONS.

6

The Eternal Child

"Return to childhood. . . . recover its truth, its vision, its logic, its sense of time and space, its extraordinary cosmology, and its creative physics if we want a way out of the black-and-white world of disenchantment."

—Thomas Moore,
The Re-Enchantment of Everyday Life

When John was born, I started a journal. It was to be a gift to him when he got older. It chronicles my feelings and reflections, and it details the growth and learning that we both experienced during this time. It is filled with the things John loved to do and talks about our first connecting together. Looking at this journal now allows me to return to the colorful, enchanting world of his childhood.

> You love being outside. You enjoy walking on the sidewalk in front of our house, going all the way to the corner and back at a good gait, and with a little hop to your walk. When you see the neighbor's cat "Clyde," you let out a squeal and dash quickly to him. A favorite pastime is looking out our front window to watch the activity on our busy city street. When a car or truck passes by, you quickly scream "dar...." Every Monday morning, we wait for the garbage trucks to come. You love to watch the men throw the cans and bags into the back of the truck. You wave furiously, and eye them from the window as long as they are in sight. When the weather is nicer, we go outside to watch close up, as soon as we hear the sound of their truck grinding away.... You're crazy about the "wawa" fountain in our playground park and will spend hours filling containers, drinking from the rock-like stool, and getting soaked.... At snacktime, you run toward the kitchen when you hear the word "kix," and prefer "beer," a mixture of club soda and apple juice, with your friends next door, Red and "Pot-Pot.".... Although you first trem-

bled at the sight of the vacuum, you now follow the "pusher" around the entire house with great delight.

It has been said that "heaven is a state of mind when the heart is open." The child is the closest thing we have to the eternal. Return to their world and experience its treasures.

CHILDREN ARE EXPERTS IN ENCHANTMENT.
TAKE TIME TO LOOK THROUGH THEIR EYES.

7

Change

"There is no holding of a relationship to a single form. This is not tragedy but part of the recurrent miracle of life and growth. All living relationships are in the process of change, of expansion, and must perpetually be building themselves new forms. . . .

We have so little faith in the ebb and flow of life, of love, of relationships. We insist on permanence, on duration, on continuity; when the only continuity possible in life, as in love, is in growth, in fluidity. Perhaps this is the most important thing for me to take back from beach-living: simply the memory that each cycle of the tide is valid."

—Anne Morrow Lindbergh, *Gift from the Sea*

The relationship between parent and child is a special one. Let it grow and flow. Be open to changes. Each tide can bring new discoveries. Admit the change. Ask yourself: What is the happiest moment in your life? What is the saddest time of your life? What happened to make you laugh the most? What was the most magical moment of your life? These questions help you stay connected through the change. You may have different answers—discoveries—during different tides.

Remember, all relationships build new forms. "Each cycle of
the tide is valid." Be open to ever-flowing relationships with
your children. Most family cultures discourage openness and
change. But there is a sense of peace that comes from the ever-
changing tides. Unlock the door to change. Share in the discoveries. Witness the peace.

AS EVER-CHANGING AS THE OCEAN SHOULD
BE OUR EVER-FLOWING RELATIONSHIPS
WITH OUR CHILDREN.

PART II

Caring for the Seed

8

The Seed

"From her face I could see that she relished the pace of the work world.

'Mom, you must have been terribly bored staying at home when I was a child,' I said.

'Bored? Housework is boring. But you were never boring.'

I didn't believe her, so I pressed. 'Surely children are not as stimulating as a career.'

'A career is stimulating,' she said. 'I'm glad I had one. But a career is like an open balloon. It remains inflated only as long as you keep pumping. A child is a seed. You water it. You care for it the best you can. And then it grows all by itself into a beautiful flower.'"

—New York Times, Suzanne Chazin

Patience, nurturing, and attention to cultivation will yield a sturdy child. Try to take some time each day (at least fifteen minutes, say) to play and connect one-on-one with each of your children. During this time, let your child take the lead. If your son wants you to go under the bed and hide so the bad prince won't find you, then go under the bed. If your daughter wants you to dress her doll up to be an evil black ghost and make a deadly potion for everyone to drink, then whip up a wicked outfit and mix up that drink! Whether it's a six-year-old talking about his dinosaurs, or a ten-year-old talking about her collection of stuffed animals, get involved and follow their lead. Talk about a different dinosaur. Tell a story about your favorite stuffed animal as a child. Do whatever it takes to share and connect.

My fifteen-year-old loves to talk about computers and the latest equipment. Since I am fairly illiterate on this subject, I need to get up to speed about his passion in order to have interesting conversations with him. It's a challenge keeping up with the newest computer "stuff" out there. My thirteen-year-old loves coins and basketball cards, two more things I know little about. So I do some reading about different money and its value, and I scan the sports page in the paper.

One night when I was tucking James into bed, he said he didn't get his special, one-on-one time yet. I could tell that trying to deter him until the next day was going to be tough. He wanted to teach my husband and me the macarena! So we flowed with it, and he had us doing the steps with the music blasting for the next fifteen minutes! The benefits of this special time are numerous. You will discover your children's needs, especially their emotional and psychological needs. Your listening skills will deepen and improve. Best of all, your relationship will deepen into greater warmth, kindness, closeness, and openness as you cultivate the seed of your child's inner essence.

PLAY TOTALLY WITH EACH OF YOUR
CHILDREN FOR FIFTEEN MINUTES A DAY.

9

Establishing
D.E.A.R. Time

At the beginning of the school year Thomas came home from first grade talking about "D.E.A.R." time. It means "Drop Everything And Read." His teachers had introduced the idea that every day, a short period of time should be set aside for reading. It is a time when school activities stop, and children open a book of their choice and simply read it.

Stopping for D.E.A.R. time is difficult because of the electronic distractions everywhere in the average home. Long ago, before audio and video equipment, computers, and telephones dominated most home settings, reading was the entertainment of choice in most families. It is time to bring it back.

When children are small, parents can read to them, snuggling together. As children get older, parents and children can read quietly next to one another. The key is that everyone stop what they're doing once a day and read, individually or together. Parents can read a long book aloud over a period of time. Older children can take on the reading role too. Families can decide which books they want to read out loud together, with everyone keeping an eye open to future selections. Not only does D.E.A.R. time encourage reading, but it also promotes bringing the family together to share a common activity.

❊

FAMILIES CAN BECOME CLOSER IF
THEY DROP EVERYTHING AND READ.

10

Mooing at Cows
and Pure Play

I regularly take walks along a country road that runs next to a cow pasture. Anyone who comes along with me is in for a big surprise. I moo at the cows and try to get them to talk back. I'm rather proud of my authentic "moo," even though the cows usually respond with a blank stare. I think they are trying to figure out if I am a person or a cow. Sometimes they stare for a very long time, especially if I moo again. Sometimes I get a moo back. This only encourages me further.

This cow talk is like parenting. It's best to forget yourself. In the same way, catch the child's feeling or thought while it's happening and become part of it. Become the child. Parent from your heart and let your parenting flow. Live on their side for a while. Go ahead. Just try mooing loudly. Be mischievous.

Moo again. Catch yourself becoming a cow. Catch yourself becoming a child. See the world through your child's eyes. Look deeply and hold their hand tightly. Concentrate on freeing yourself and your mind. Focus completely on the child.

Recreation, or play, means to re-create. Ask yourself "what do I do when I play?" Does it strengthen my insides? Is the joy so great that I can experience the beauty of creating and re-creating? Play is not business, not obligation, not something that has to be done, not necessarily productive, and not necessarily involved with something "worthwhile." There are times for these things, but they are not play.

Play is pure joy. My eight-year-old constantly reminds me of what play is. When he runs with delight, he expresses a rare form of joy. When he screams with enthusiasm at the plan to stay overnight at a friend's house, he expresses the same pure joy. When he races to one end of the living room, slides, leaps up, runs back, and slides again, he is playing. Play means to laugh, jump, celebrate, and feel happy. If you don't look forward to your play, there is no joy in it.

Most people will reply to the question "what do you do for fun?" by listing all the planned activities on their calendar. They are going to go to the health club after work, then out to dinner with a friend, then to their daughter's basketball game, then to the symphony with their friends. These are very important activities, but they aren't pure play unless you look forward to them because they bring you happy feelings, fill you up with joy, and make you smile. An empty calendar can bring such a feeling. It leaves the door open for your day to flow naturally, playfully.

So how does one begin to play? It helps to turn off the TV and the computer. Get outside. Connect to nature. Experience the beauty of our earth. Look around and feel a part of the joy and wisdom of what you see. Walk, run, move physically. Stop thinking. Start really looking at what you see. Start feeling. Balance heart thoughts with head thoughts. Let out intuition. FLOW. Allow play to emerge. See what comes out to play. Try not to force play. Be spontaneous. Laugh. Open up a new capacity for fun. Let go. Free your own child within. Enjoy the now. Do nothing. Observe the quiet. Just be together. Dance! Try mooing at cows.

Here are some family play ideas that work for us:

+ Try the "blank canvas" project (see page 148). It involves the entire family painting together on a single canvas with each member selecting a portion of it. Do this once a year. Be sure to date it. Looking back and comparing the annual art reveals where the family was during those years together.

+ Play baseball or basketball as a team, or break into several smaller teams that challenge one another.

+ Play a wild game of cards with poker chips. (Sometimes we use pennies.) Everyone has to wear gambling visors.

+ Go to an outdoor concert and take a picnic basket along. Don't forget your special blanket.

+ Dance with each other.

+ Sing loudly together.

+ Watch the sun set together. (Be sure you catch it as it "sinks.")

+ Focus on the sky. Measure the width of the full moon. Find different constellations at night. Find different animal shapes in the clouds, and share your whimsical findings with each other.

+ Establish special Dad play days. These are times when just Dad takes the children on an outing. These Dad days encourage unusual activities in our family.
+ Have one-on-one play days where one child gets all the attention and chooses the agenda from a list of fun possibilities.

LET GO AND PLAY!

Hammock Time
and the Shade Tree

There is tremendous value in what I call "hammock time." This means doing nothing. Daydreaming, hanging out, getting lost in your thoughts, doodling. Call it what you will, it means shifting gears to neutral, forgetting to speed ahead in third or fourth gear. Our culture puts so much emphasis on *doing*, and children soon pick that up. Then they start doing all those "achieve and succeed" things—from math tests to music recitals—which, more often than not, bring on way too much pressure.

As parents, it is vitally important for us to allow children to have this special hammock time. Children, like adults, are nourished by introspective time to wonder and dream. Open time is essential for all of us, but especially for children. It provides a balance in their lives. If a week is extremely hectic for a child or parent and "doing nothing" over the weekend is preferred, then respect this need and do it. Forget about the menu of suggested activities for Saturday.

Give your child a "shade tree." If you don't have a yard, choose a tree in the park or open an umbrella and pretend. If you have a yard, find a special spot, a quiet place where your child can sit and grow. It becomes his learning tree. Under this tree, children discover their strengths. They have special dreams and gifts that must be cared for and nurtured. Their strengths can be fed and watered under the shade tree. Children need help keeping their strengths visible. They need to be told and reminded of their delicious fruit. It is a peculiar fact—we all tend to forget what we're good at doing! The shade tree lets us return to reflect on our fruit, to check whether it has ripened.

Besides a quiet place, the shade tree gives children a place to reflect. It is here that they can do a "self-check" on their personal growth. They can discover and learn what is best for them. They can experience feelings of competence and independence. Imagine, doing all of this just sitting under a tree!

FOCUS ON DOING NOTHING
AND ALLOW YOUR CHILD
TO WONDER AND DREAM.
LET YOUR CHILD SIT ALONE
IN A HAMMOCK OR UNDER A SHADE TREE
AND EXPERIENCE SOLITUDE.

12

Frog Races and Summertime

We have a lot of frogs in our area, so we decided to have annual summer frog races. We spend a lot of fun time finding the frogs and toads, and then we put them in a large window sill near a basement, where they are cool and happy. We feel sure they enjoy the company of the other frogs until, of course, the races begin. The collecting of these special frogs takes from several days to a week. Frogs don't suddenly appear and say "take me!" It takes time, especially night time, to locate them. Some are large and others are small. Surface spots, skin colors, and textures vary. Each of us begins to eye the one we'd like to enter in the race. Strong attachments unavoidably occur. When you get really involved, their eyes communicate back to you.

We've learned from previous years what kinds of frogs move the fastest. One would expect large frogs to really zoom, but we've discovered that the little ones are the quickest. Since this is a test for speed, we've also discovered how to assist them in their movement. It's one of those little techniques that has incredible impact on the race's outcome. When you blow gently on the frog's back end, it will leap. This requires you to stay low to the ground and behind it, and jump along too, especially if it really gets moving. We have one rule during the frog's travel:

you cannot pick up or touch the frog with your hands (or feet) at any point in the race.

Prizes are very important. We go to the local store and pick out our favorite kind of bubble gum and different colored Tootsie Roll pops. Every entrant must receive a prize. Fanfare is created for the first-, second-, and third-place winners; they receive larger items, also from the all-too-sweet category. We chalk out very clear start and finish lines, usually about twenty feet apart. Frogs turn as they "race" ahead. They really don't think in terms of forward, nor onward, so the length of the race can't be any longer. As in any race, cheering is also important, but this noise can create puzzlement to the frogs, so it must be discrete and very carefully expressed.

You can also have turtle races if you can find "wild" turtles. It is really hard to locate them in their natural surroundings because they don't make sounds, are well camouflaged in both water and land, and are great hiders. Turtle races require a shorter course, about fifteen feet in length. Again, entrants are not allowed to touch the turtles during the race. This rule means you can't pick them up and turn them toward the finish line when they're traveling the wrong way. We've discovered that your physical presence may get them to change direction, and this can work as your best strategy. Standing in front of their path can sometimes keep them on track, but it can also cause them to turn and head away from the finish line. Pick-ing the winning turtle can be unpredictable, but the corny prizes, enthusiastic cheering, and endless laughter are key ingredients to successful "racing" outcomes. Try it!

HOOKING UP WITH NATURE
PROMISES LEARNING AND DISCOVERY FOR
CHILDREN AND ADULTS ALIKE.

13

On Teenagers and Toads

I thought I knew my two oldest sons extremely well since I've lived with them for the past fifteen years. But only recently have I discovered that a new and unique species inhabits our home—teenagers. After observing their behaviors, I can clearly see that teenagers and toads share some unique qualities.

During the summer I get the opportunity to spend a great deal of time with both groups. Once school is out, our family heads to the country for four weeks. There are three frog-filled ponds located in the field next to us. With two of my three children now officially teenagers, my hunch regarding the similarities between teenagers and toads has been confirmed. While each is distinctively unique, they have a number of common features.

Both groups sleep long hours and are nocturnal creatures. Toads hibernate for long periods during the winter months. Teenagers can easily snooze ten to twelve hours a day, sometimes thirteen. Considerable noise and activity during the night is quite common. Need I say more about teenage night-noise?

They even move alike. Toads make unexpected jumps. You can't tell which way they will go, or when they're going to make a move. Teenagers have this element of unpredictability about their behavior too. Often, it is impossible to tell how they are going to react. They may say "no way" to something and then be jubilant when you decide to go ahead with it anyway. One thing is for sure—their moves are erratic and they're difficult to catch.

Toads are amphibians. The word *amphibian* means "two lives." Toads and frogs were the first four-legged, backboned creatures to walk on land and survive out of water. Teenagers also have two lives. They are in transition between childhood and adulthood. Much of their energy is focused on shedding the ways of children and evolving into adults.

Toads experience an unusual metamorphosis. Watching a tadpole grow to an adult frog is an incredible sight. Its head and body become distinct, and its legs pop out—first hind legs, then front legs. The tail slowly grows shorter and all but disappears. Teenagers' bodies experience a similar metamorphosis. Half-tadpole, half-frog bodies are comparable to the teenagers' half-child, half-adult bodies. Both groups are physically transitioning into something else.

Toads have considerable expertise in camouflaging themselves to the color of their surroundings. To conceal themselves from predators, they hide in ground cover; but in open areas, they make "dugouts" and burrow into the ground until danger has passed. Teenagers also engage in a type of burrowing. They are very conscious of their surroundings, especially when other people are watching them. In particular, they burrow or get out of sight when they don't want to be seen at a public event with their parents. Concealment from their parents is important.

We can't take this personally. Equate it to nothing more than a toad wanting to be safe from its predators.

Eating habits are similar between teenagers and toads. The majority of amphibians are carnivores. Most gulp down spiders, insects, earthworms, and other types of crawlers—ants, snails, and slugs. They will gorge themselves when food is abundant in order to survive when food is scarce. Witness the ornate horned toad with its huge mouth and camouflaged body. After catching a large prey, this toad blinks its eyes repeatedly to increase the pressure in its mouth, assisting it in swallowing its meal. Teenagers approach snacks and meals with equal vigor. They can handle big mouthfuls too and swallow large quantities of food with ease, fully in control of their movements.

Toads are great fun to watch. Their unusual physical features alone make viewing a sport. They have bumpy skin, their eyes change shape and color, and their long stretchy legs are always ready for jumping maneuvers. Teenagers are fun to watch, too. As parents, we could do more watching. Why not focus on observing and accepting their unique qualities, strengths, and extraordinary characteristics? We need to value our teenagers' genuine individualities. Most parents fiddle with and want to change their emerging teens. But success is achieved only if we let teenagers grow up according to their own schedules, in their own ways. Let teens make contact with their own "insides," and help build their self-esteem.

To me, listening to toads and frogs around a pond on a summer night is the most glorious, harmonious symphony one will ever hear. As my teenager says, when something meets with his complete approval, the sound is "so sweet." When our children were little, I took them to a workshop at a nearby nature center. We learned how to make the sounds of four different toads and frogs. After considerable practice, we were each assigned one frog call to imitate for audiotaping. I was a spring peeper and my sons were bull frogs. The recording session was our big debut! When our tape was played back and compared to the sounds of a summer night pond scene, there was a remarkable resemblance to the sounds. Likewise, as parents we need to listen deeply to our teens. Get to know their sounds so well that you can play them back.

APPRECIATE THE INNATE BEAUTY, MYSTERY, AND JOY OF TEENS. IT CAN TRULY BE A "RIBBET-ING" EXPERIENCE.

14

The Little Things

"I look back on our lunchtimes together, bathed in the soft midday light. They were the commas in my childhood, the pauses that told me life is not savored in premeasured increments, but in the sum of daily rituals and small pleasures we casually share with loved ones. Over peanut-butter sandwiches and chocolate-chip cookies, I learned that love, first and foremost, means being there for the little things."

—*New York Times*, Suzanne Chazin

Parents can get so busy juggling their children's schedules and their own work and social schedules that they forget to get involved in the "little" things of their children's lives. Slow down and savor those moments together. Limit the outside activities after school. Come home instead and build a fire, listen to it crackle, and drink hot chocolate together. SLOW DOWN.

I wrote these ideas down one day, and I call them the big lessons little children can teach us when we take it more slowly. It's good to revisit them frequently. They are:

+ Focus on the present—stop doing.
+ Observe your children's growth.
+ Enjoy their presence.
+ Listen quietly too.
+ Observe their body language.
+ Check their strengths. Does self-esteem shine?
+ Know their needs now. Anticipate what they will need later.
+ Add hugs.
+ Connect with one another.
+ Try to keep things simple.
+ Give your heart, not your advice.
+ Be available, present, open.
+ Establish a spirit of kindness.
+ Enjoy your life together.
+ Be open to what might be possible.
+ See your children slowly forming, then blooming.

In order for each child to grow properly, you must turn off the television. Pull the plug on the computer. They distract us from a child's growth, like some big noisy fly buzzing about, landing on all signs of life. Appreciate the stillness. Walk in the garden together. Invite learning. Be open to what their path teaches us. There is an inner experience to parenting. We should seek to know ourselves better and discover our place as parents in the child's garden. A radiant flower can emerge—its beauty totally unperceived until the day it blooms. Perhaps all

we can do as parents is watch our children deeply, listen to them happily, and walk together through their garden with kindness and love.

SLOW DOWN AND SAVOR THE LITTLE THINGS
WITH YOUR CHILD.

Part III

Creating
the
Pattern

15

The Quilter's Lesson

Several summers ago, we visited an Amish farm. There we saw a woman well into her eighties meticulously working on a quilt. Her careful eye focused intently on the quality of each tiny piece of fabric, only about one-half inch wide. These individual squares, sewn together by hand, would eventually create the completed quilt. Altogether, she said it would take two thousand squares. She perfected each individual patch with diligence and concern. In this way, she worked on the "inside" of the quilt, much like a watchful parent develops the "inside" of a child. The seamstress gives careful attention to the developing quilt; the parent gives detailed and encouraging information to the child. Both are watchful. One sews a sturdy quilt; the other cultivates a vibrant child.

This Amish woman told us that it would take her five thousand hours to complete the entire quilt. On the day we visited, she began at 8:00 in the morning and was still working at 3:00 in the afternoon. She managed to spend about four hours daily, six days a week, leaving Sunday for worship. At this rate, her quilt-making project would extend over four years.

The completed quilt is magnificent, as is the glory and beauty of the young adult. Both take large amounts of time. Over the years, one weaves together family activities to create a unique culture, just as one sews individual squares together to create a magnificent quilt. One builds a family of self-reliant individuals with inner confidence and varied strengths, just as one creates a colorful and beautifully integrated quilt for all to behold. In this section, I will tell you about some of the "notions" I have found most useful in weaving the fabric of our family's togetherness. They are:

W   for Watch

E   for Encourage

A   for Appreciate

V   for Visualize

E   for Empathize

ALL THE THREADS—A FAMILY'S ACTIONS,
VALUES, EVENTS, COMMUNICATIONS, AND
TRADITIONS—ARE LACED TIGHTLY
TOGETHER TO CREATE SOMETHING
SUSTAINING AND STRONG—A CULTURE
THAT ENFOLDS THE ENTIRE FAMILY.

16

"W" for Watch

Just like the weaver watches the astonishing detail of the pattern emerge, parents can look for the amazing details of each child. By paying close attention, parents can help their children see, respect, and value their own inner strengths. I think this is their most important job. But how do you help your child see her bright colors, her unique strengths? *Reflect back what you see.*

Use the power of affirmations or statements of praise—the more specific, the better. Most praise is too general and, because of this, doesn't build self-esteem. Many parents will simply say, "You look great" or "You did a terrific job on that assignment." Their praise is generic; they've forgotten to add any specific information. A child needs to hear that she is wonderful, *and why.*

Put a WOW in your voice and praise with enthusiasm.
Try out a new level of enthusiasm now. The difference in its
impact will totally surprise you! Praise is not something given
occasionally or on a part-time basis, but continuously, every
chance you get. And don't wait to extend your praise. Give it
quickly or soon after it is due.

Each child has qualities inside them that need to be
pointed out. It may take this form: "James, I love spending time
with you because you . . . (list some qualities) . . . have a funny
sense of humor, I feel we can talk about anything, you are very
observant and have good people sense, and I can sing 'oldies'
really loud when you're around!" Now what happens to this

child if he is told—frequently—that he makes you laugh, communicates openly, has good insight into people, and encourages you to sing, even when you can't carry a tune? He most likely does not get this verbal information from his peers, his siblings, or most of the adults with whom he interacts. If he hears it over and over from a significant adult, he is more likely to absorb this information. People who know their strengths, who are aware of their unique qualities, become stronger and more confident. The ultimate goal is for a child to be secure in her own abilities and no longer dependent on the opinion of others. This person can say "I do these things well," and believe it!

WATCH

FOR OPPORTUNITIES TO BUILD YOUR CHILD'S
CONFIDENCE WITH LOTS OF SPECIFIC AND
ENTHUSIASTIC PRAISE.

17

"E" for Encourage

Besides using specific information in their praise, encouraging parents store it. They know when their child has done something particularly well. They can recall, for example, when their child managed to share her thoughts at just the right time, was able to remember critical details during an emergency situation, helped find a solution to a problem, or came up with a new idea. The encouraging parent knows these fine points or circumstances and can recall the necessary specific information from the child's past. This parent can say, "Remember when you helped your friend find her lost term paper by walking her through her stops after school? I know you can backtrack to find your new gloves in the same way."

Think of a parent as the child's resource librarian, keeping the child's past accomplishments and achievements within their "shelves." They share this information with their child and provide encouragement and comfort when necessary, but especially during difficult times of growth and frustration. In this way, they help a child discover his or her inner resources, sometimes located deep within. In this way, they can help the child do the more difficult, life-integrating work too.

For example, when a child has been criticized by someone outside the family, the encouraging parent can help "take out the garbage" by identifying whatever aspects might be unfair or untrue, reminding the child of her strengths, then offering a plan that remedies the situation. If your child is criticized for sloppy handwriting, she needs to practice the letters on the same line. If told she has poor math skills, then she needs more drill. If told she behaves rudely, then she needs to practice waiting for others to finish before speaking. If told her planning is not thorough, then she needs to put more focus and detail into future plans. If told these same plans don't include the interests of everyone involved, then she needs to build in the ideas of others. If parents can think through what specific action needs to be taken to help the child, then a strong and spirited young adult can emerge.

ENCOURAGE

YOUR CHILDREN BY STORING UP THEIR
STRENGTHS AND ACCOMPLISHMENTS FOR A
RAINY DAY.

18

"A" for Appreciate Differences

Just as each pattern has a varied and different look, children's intelligence is varied too. There is a magical quality to the study of intelligence, if we broaden our definition of it. Imagine waving a magic wand and turning everyone into super-intelligent beings. The truth is not too far off. Everyone is smart—just in different ways.

Parents must know that there are different kinds of intelligence. An IQ score measures intelligence with words and numbers. It provides the traditional definition of ability. It says a child is smart if she can read a story and understand what happened or do advanced math calculations with ease. SAT scores reflect these more traditional types of intelligence, but such tests actually restrict the definition of intelligence.

Ask yourself if you think of these people as intelligent: The mechanic who quickly identified why your car wouldn't run, the little girl next door who wrote a moving poem about how much she liked your grandmother, the friend who can understand why you feel the way you do before you share your thoughts, the young band member who can play four instruments and quickly sing a new song by looking at the musical score, the boy who enjoys taking things apart and putting them back together, the ten-year-old who can observe an unusual bird and draw it from memory several days later, the five-year-old who can easily dribble the ball down the court and make a basket. The truth is that *all* of these people are smart, but they express their intelligence differently.

Howard Gardner, co-director of Project Zero at Harvard University, has broadened the definition of intelligence to include seven areas:

1. **Musical intelligence**, which means being able to sing on key, maintain a beat, remember music that has been heard, or compose and read songs.

2. **Interpersonal intelligence or social ability**, which means having a strong ability to enjoy friends and groups and their activities; to perceive people's moods, temperaments, motivations, and intentions; and to display empathy.

3. **Spatial intelligence**, which means having good visual memory or the ability to find one's way around, read maps, take things apart and reassemble them, or work with paints, design, light, or architectural drawings.

4. **Intrapersonal intelligence**, which means being deeply aware of one's own feelings and thoughts, and being able to recognize and discriminate among these feelings. These people are aware of what they love and fear, are able to insightfully talk about their own experiences, and have an unusual understanding of themselves.

5. **Bodily-kinesthetic intelligence**, which means demonstrating coordination, ability, and skill in both fine and gross motor movements, as with a craftsperson or athlete.

6. **Linguistic intelligence**, which means using language to communicate written and spoken meanings—to write and read. It also includes being able to word-play, rhyme, tell stories, and enjoy puns.

7. **Logico-mathematical intelligence**, which means thinking conceptually; reasoning; devising experiments; exploring abstract relationships in math, computers and logic; and noticing patterns and numbers in their environment.

Taken together, these types of intelligence provide seven ways to learn. They broaden our definition of intelligence, and in so doing, free a child. Parents must learn what kind of intelligences their children have in order to nurture and strengthen them.

APPRECIATE

THAT ALL CHILDREN ARE SMART—JUST IN
VARIED AND MAGICAL WAYS.

19

"V" for Visualize

Think about the finished cloth or woven blanket. It's soft and finally big enough so that it can cover you up. You can pull it over you to keep warm during the night or on a cold afternoon. As parents, we can become too "tough" and too focused on the child's mistakes. Keep the soft, finished blanket in mind. Our children will "finish" too, and become fully grown adults.

If you would like a child to change, think of him as already having the qualities that you would like him to have. Visualize your child as a dependable, capable, and reliable adult, and interact with him as if he were already what you would like him to become. Holding this image helps us not to get hung up on all the mistakes along the way, but to focus instead on enjoying the journey itself, knowing that the end—a responsible, mature, and caring adult—will be realized in due time.

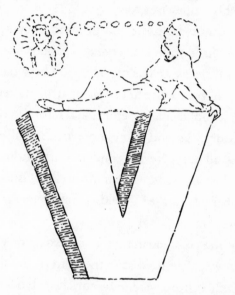

Keeping the end in mind can really help, because the trip is an adventurous one! There will be times when a child is undependable or a poor student. One of our sons has entered this zone. Not too long ago, he was unusually dependable personally and excellent academically. It was quite a shock to us. We've learned to focus on the knowledge that he is *in the process* of becoming a more dependable and capable adult. He's just taking a little detour. He's exploring and experimenting. This is good. My husband and I must remind ourselves that his experimentation serves as a teacher. He will uncover and learn more of himself on his pathway to adulthood, and we will learn more about ourselves too.

When parents keep the end in mind, they don't overfocus on all the little things. Everyday a family has to balance thousands of little, as well as big, things. These include work, money, and car problems; house or apartment repairs; meal preparation; school demands; emotional setbacks; relationship paths and roadblocks; and many more kinds of all-consuming issues. These all compete for time and attention within the family circle. Just as the weaver stands back to visualize the finished fabric, parents can see a child's pattern emerge within the family culture.

Choose the color, structure, and texture of your family pattern, then visualize it. Watch the pattern unfold and ask: Does our family culture need to be enriched? Does the pattern need a different line here or more color there? Is our family culture missing an opportunity for this or not spending enough time on that? Does the fabric need to add more stripes and plaids or a new rib weave? Does our family focus enough on building friendships, teaching children to talk, care, share, love, and learn? Should we add yarns with softer texture and will these make a difference in how they need to be handled? Does our family talk about what brings them sadness or pain? Does the fabric require stronger or wider yarns? Are family members each giving and receiving love? Is the cloth large enough to cover us as we grow?

So, like the weaver, stand back. Visualize what you want your culture to become. If you don't have enough time together, how can you change your family? You have to be happy with it. You have to feel good about what you're weaving together. Create a pattern. Be inventive and make it different, if you want. It can be vibrant and outspoken, or soft and quiet. Make it alive and choose special colors. Walk hand-in-hand. Collaborate on the pattern. Get passionate about it. Make it ageless. Learn to think like a child again—climb high in the tree and sit up there in the blue sky. If you do, you will more fully experience and find joy in the present. And you'll catch a glimpse of the child and her emerging adult and know it's not too far away.

VISUALIZE

THE CHILD AND HER FAMILY CULTURE IN
THEIR END-STATE, AND FIND COMFORT FROM
THIS VIEW.

20

"E" for Empathize

Parents must learn to read feelings. Put yourself in your child's shoes. Discover that your child is upset and worried because the book is too difficult to read. Understand that your older child is sad because a friend didn't get accepted into the program. Learn that your child's distress comes from the fact that only one goldfish remains in the bowl, and this goldfish must be painstakingly cared for so that it will live a long life!

Feelings reflect reality. They emerge from inside the child and become invaluable information. To honor a child's feelings is to understand and strengthen that child. Sometimes, all children need to know is that someone else is aware of how they feel and why. Acknowledging their feelings—expressing empathy—may be all that is necessary to fix a hurt.

Though they mean well, most adults attempt to counter a child's feelings. They deny, dismiss, and ignore them, or worse—try to talk them out of having their feelings. Take a close look at the words you use when your children share their feelings. *How to Talk So Kids Can Learn* is one of my favorite books. Its authors, Adele Faber and Elaine Mazlish, identify a mixture of typical parent responses to children's feelings. Using their categories, I take the example below of a high school boy who feels bad because he didn't make the football team. Different words and approaches are used with this distraught boy. Do you recognize some of your own responses?

+ **Denial of Feelings:** "You shouldn't feel so bad. Don't get so upset. The world won't end just because you didn't make the team."

+ **The Philosophical Response:** "Don't think about it; learn to roll with the punches; life can be unfair."

+ **Advice:** "Don't let this get you down. You can try out for another team."

+ **Too Many Questions:** "Do you think the coach made a mistake? Why would they cut you? Do you know other kids who were cut?"

+ **Defense of the Other Person:** "Maybe the coach had a good reason. Maybe there were too many who went out for the team."

+ **Amateur Psychoanalysis:** "Maybe on a subconscious level you had real self doubts about your abilities, so you just didn't play well."

+ **Pity:** "You poor thing. You tried so hard to make the team. All the other kids know you didn't make it, and you must feel so embarrassed."

These are examples of typical parent talk, but Faber and Mazlish also outline four ways to acknowledge children's feelings. I like them because they help expand the repertoire of choices available to parents. A sample response is given with each category, using the same example of the boy who was cut from the football team.

1. **Instead of denying their feelings, put them into words.** "Oh . . . what a disappointment. You were really looking forward to being on the team!"

2. **Acknowledge the child's feelings with words or sounds.** "Oh" or "I see" or "Mmm" express concern and understanding. These simple responses can serve to free the child to figure out how to deal with the issue himself. The child is able to think about the problem, take responsibility for it, and possibly reach a solution.

3. **Give the child in fantasy what you can't give him in reality.** "Wouldn't it be great if you practiced kicking the football on your own after school and were able to join the team later in the season as a backup kicker when your skills improve."

4. **Accept the child's feelings even as you stop unacceptable behavior.** "I know you're so mad at the coach for cutting you from the team that you'd like to trip him in the hallway the next time you see him. You can't do anything physical like that, but you could ask him to put you on the list to practice with the team, in case some of the players don't show up."

These parent responses express openness to and acceptance of the child's true feelings. They show that the parent has learned to read the child and respond with openness. As parents, we need to expand our responses when our children share their feelings. Empathy is critical in weaving closeness between family members.

EMPATHIZE
WITH YOUR CHILD'S FEELINGS.

21

Familyweaving

When Thomas was in first grade, he brought home a sheet of paper that displayed his first attempts at writing. He had drawn and colored a picture of a very cold person who was dressed for extreme snow conditions, but was still shivering and had chattering teeth. Under the picture he had written the words: "I think it is willy willy code. I think hes in the noth poie and I think he is willy willy code."

Teachers call these early attempts at word making "inventive spelling." At this stage of learning, it is important *not* to correct the child's spelling because he is sounding out the words and inventing his own construction of them. To suggest that he change the spelling of "willy willy code" to "really, really cold" at this point can stifle his interest and enthusiasm and actually impede his progress. We put his writing up on our refrigerator and still smile whenever we see it.

Learning to write is like familyweaving. To insist on the final result at the very beginning would be a mistake. To insist that the child be at the journey's end when she is still developing and growing would also be wrong. Although keeping the end in mind helps us to keep perspective and be patient, we should not be too focused on the finish line.

In the same way that spelling begins with learning the sounds of letters and their combinations, familyweaving begins with learning about the child. Each child has remarkable gifts. Children naturally extend these gifts when adults let them. Unfortunately, adults too often control the off/on button for their expression. Yet, if we listen to the voices of our children, they can teach us a great deal about parenting, just as when we listen to the letters' sounds, they teach us how to spell the word.

IT TAKES TIME AND PATIENCE TO WEAVE A
CLOSE FAMILY.

PART IV

Communicating

22

The Vegetable Garden
and Connecting

Late every spring we plant a vegetable garden. We do this project as a family. When we first started, six years ago, we weren't really sure how to go about it, but now it all flows together. We don't have to talk much about it, nor think much either. We just automatically do it together. When we plant our vegetable garden, certain things need to be done. Among the five of us, everyone now can do every task that is needed.

We prepare the soil by rototilling it several times. Stirring the soil is great fun. Everyone usually wants a turn behind the rototiller machine. We add cow manure and peat to enrich the soil, mixing it into the "old" earth from last year. Then we pick out the seeds and plants from the local nursery. This involves much family decision making, since each of us has a favorite

vegetable or two. We are open to trying new kinds of vegetables, especially if they have unusual physical features, and we
spend quite a lot of time watching our plants grow. (Brussels
sprouts, broccoli, and cabbage fall into the interesting-to-
watch-grow category.) But we also love going back to the same
tried-and-true vegetables.

After deciding which vegetables to buy, we bring them
back and plan their placement in the garden. We've learned
that vegetables, like people, prefer certain neighbors to others.
We know, for example, that carrots love cabbage. We believe
that planting them next to one another is very important for
their growth and "happiness." Most of our decisions are based

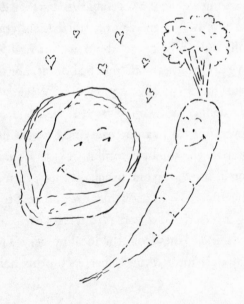

on history—where we planted them last year and how well they did. Once a location has been tested one year and proved a success, we reserve the same space again for the next year. Pole beans always get put in the same corner to climb up our teepee-like structure. The pepper corner is occupied by five different kinds and colors of peppers. They are next to the cucumbers, which are next to the zucchini, the yellow squash, and the winter squash. We also have an experimental area where we try out new kinds of vegetables. Radishes, nasturtiums, and sunflowers surround the garden, and herbs are planted in the center. When we give tours of our garden, we proudly point out the location of each individual vegetable.

All the different kinds of vegetables join together to create this magnificent chorus of color and bounty. We love to watch it grow and change. We nurture it with water. The sun adds its energy. And the vegetables ripen with time. I haven't said too much about eating the vegetables, although we *do* thoroughly enjoy the meals from our freshly picked crops. But it is growing together as a family that is the basic joy of our garden.

Growing together involves building relationships, and this requires knowing the personal strengths and needs of each family member. It is sort of like deciding whether potatoes or pumpkins would grow better and why. You have to learn each vegetable's strengths. Growing together also involves celebrating the independence of each person. And that is sort of like celebrating cucumbers for their qualities, which are separate from the qualities of strawberries or rhubarb. Becoming closer as a family is an end in itself. It is much like the vegetable garden, where eating the "goods" isn't all that's important. It's the process of growing them that provides the most joy and satisfaction. I am reminded every year that families, like gardens, create something powerful and rich through their relationships.

WORKING TOGETHER ON FAMILY PROJECTS
NOURISHES AND DEEPENS THE FAMILY.

23

The Hummingbird
and Giving

Teach your children the importance of service. Help them learn ways to be of service to their friends, their family, and their school- and playmates. Teach them to dedicate a portion of their life to a larger purpose. Help them believe they can make a significant difference, first, within themselves, and then in the world. Ghandi taught us that we must *be* the change that we wish to see in the world.

Look, for example, at the hummingbird, an amazing little creature. I like to watch it float above the sage bush in our backyard. It is a beautiful, colorful bird and makes this unusual little squeaky sound. It flies with tremendous accuracy and speed. But you don't see it very often because of its swift patterns. It goes around to all the flowers and takes out their sweet nectar, which it spreads, pollinating other flowers. Unless you catch it near the flowers, you never know it has been there. Service is like that too. Even though acts of service and kindness soon vanish, their profound value to others never does. The nectar is spread. Other flowers flourish.

The hummingbird's nest is a most inspiring piece of creation. Only about two inches in diameter, it is delicate, lightweight, and made with very fine collections of animal hair, grasses, and fine straw—all stitched together as though a needle and thread had been used. The hummingbird's nest is a stunning monument to the beauty of a home, its interwoven relationships, delicately pieced together. If you ever find one of these rare nests, you've found gold. Once strong relationships have been nurtured within your family, you've discovered their treasure too. Family relationships, like the hummingbird's nest materials, can be stitched tightly together. They are the real gold of family life.

The hummingbird teaches an important lesson: Leave a legacy of giving. Make charity a major part of your life. Take your gifts—personal and professional—and enrich your community. Seek the extraordinary with your ordinary gifts. Pollinate the flowers. Make a difference in your community. Do as much as you can for others. This is how the world improves. Teach a legacy of service. Make it a personal mission. Teach a child to make the world more beautiful, like the hummingbird who pollinates the flower. It can be as simple as picking up a room or putting just one thing away before you leave it—or as difficult as speaking your mind and your conscience on a difficult topic. Teach a child how to take their individual gifts and make a significant difference in their community too. Encourage them to *be* the change that they wish to see in the world. Better yet, show them how you do this in your life.

TEACH YOUR CHILDREN TO SERVE OTHERS,
PRACTICE CHARITY, AND LEAVE
A LEGACY OF GIVING AND SHARING.

24

Deep Listening and Playing Frisbee

One evening after work, I watched a family arrive on the beach to play Frisbee. The two men began to toss the Frisbee back and forth. Given the nearby waves and their often wild throws, their work clothes became fully soaked in no time at all. Water temperature and wetness seemed to be of no concern to them. Completely intent on catching the Frisbee, to stop and put on swimsuits would have ruined their play and focus. After fifteen minutes, the mother joined in the game, followed by the child a short time later. Unhesitantly jumping into the water to make the catch, their soaked clothes stuck to their bodies, along with globs of crusted sand. Their laughter spoke louder than the sound of the waves. This family, I think, must have been good listeners. Let me explain.

Think of the speaker and listener as playing a game of Frisbee. A Frisbee can be awkward to throw accurately because of its rim and radius. Listening is like catching it. You have to really pay attention, focus on the thrower, anticipate where it is going to be thrown, be ready to leap out to catch it wherever it goes, and finally make the catch. It requires the complementary skills and efforts of both players, appropriately attuned to each other.

Look at the special roles of speaker and listener. The speaker must observe the listener attentively, looking for "indicators" as to whether she is listening. The listener must observe the speaker attentively, too, and express feelings of warmth and enthusiasm. Physical contact, even smiles, also convey good listening. While it is the role of the speaker to communicate a specific message, it is the role of the listener to receive the meaning of the words. The listener must learn, understand, retain, and finally, acknowledge that the message has been received. This deep listening is rarely experienced anymore.

An active listener will communicate that they are with you in any number of ways. Their eyes are alert, or they may nod their head. They may ask questions, verbally acknowledge that they have understood an idea, or add information. If their posture is alert, or they get closer to you physically to reduce the distance between you, or shut the door to outside noise, or ask others to join the group—then you know the listener has been busy. Good listeners may begin to apply the general information you have given them to more specific situations.

Most speakers know whether active listening has occurred. My fifteen-year-old son will abruptly stop talking when he discovers that a person is not listening. He says, "Why talk when no one seems to be listening?" Oddly, most adults will continue talking even though there are no signs that someone is listening! They have forgotten how to observe the listener.

Watching for indicators is not easy to do. If there are no questions or if eye contact is poor (e.g., looking out the window is common), then it should be clear to the speaker that two-way communication hasn't happened. Some indicators of poor communications include asking questions just for the sake of it and looking at the speaker, but not listening. Good speakers know when someone is doing this. They know when their "audience" is not there to catch their thoughts.

Remember, your main task as a listener is to understand what the speaker is trying to say and to let him know that you understand. Attitude is just as important as what you say back.

Nonverbal responses can often convey more meaningful and quicker feedback than words. Focus on and check your own listening skills. Ask yourself if you:

+ are attentive
+ accept the speaker and the situation
+ clarify and try to understand
+ see your views change or be supported
+ encourage the speaker
+ let your listening guide you

If you follow these guidelines, you will listen more deeply. And I bet you will catch a Frisbee more easily, too.

LEARN TO LISTEN ACTIVELY SO THAT YOU
CAN CATCH EACH THOUGHT.

25

Talk and Whoop

The child psychotherapist Dr. Haim Ginott in his classic book *Teacher and Child* offers guidance to teachers and parents on how to talk to children. Their language, he stresses, tells a child how they feel about her and, to a large extent, affects her self-worth and self-esteem. Their statements determine her destiny. Take a close look at your language, and remember the impact of your words.

Encourage your child to talk and talk, and listen actively too. Talking is critical to learning because it increases understanding. John Dewey, the famous educational philosopher, said that learning involves the re-presentation of one's experiences. When we encourage a child to talk in a group—family or school—the child learns. The child re-presents her experi-

ences and begins to understand them. And when a child hears
other children and adults talking, her pool of possibilities is
enlarged.

Cultivate the ability to talk about everything. Teach children the value of totally open communication. Don't restrict
the boundaries of conversation. Let them know it's good to
grow individually in different areas and directions. Always
encourage active listening and you'll learn from each other. Be
open, direct, and deep. Describe problems, give information,
encourage dialogue, and don't forget to model how to do it.
Fully express your own feelings, needs, and expectations. You
might even share your flaws. Talk about everything and nothing—from racial discrimination and its causes to favorite foods
and how you like to eat them. Share your own past experiences, good and bad, and what you learned. It will inspire your
children to share theirs, now and as they get older. Walk down
unknown conversational paths. Tell the truth. Feel safe. Let
this kind of deep talk nourish you. It will create rich and rare
friendships with your children.

Learning to talk deeply like this creates a rare and wonderful energy between you. Imagine what family settings would
be like if there was no talking. This happens in strict families.
Children are afraid to say anything, so there is silence. They
quickly learn that they must be seen and not heard. Lack of

communication exists in most families. Deep communication is rare. Yelling, the worst form, is too common. Close and healthy families are built through frequent, open, two-way talk with one another—and lots of it. Try to talk on a regular basis, especially at meals when everyone is sitting together. Establish a ritual where family members go around the table and talk about the most meaningful—or discouraging—part of their day. This may be an event at school, a personal project, or a thought—anything that has special importance. Happy as well as sad experiences can be shared during this time. Try to break free from old and repeated topics. It's good to change your conversational patterns. Open up new thoughts, dream out loud, share private tears, and explore perspectives on everything—from friends to fears. Know deep talking can be effortless, if you let it.

Don't forget to laugh and "whoop." Whooping is loud and spontaneous laughter. I am known for my loud and uncontrollable whoop, even in restaurants. People always want to know what's going on at our table. Sometimes, they start laughing. "Whoops" inspire more talk.

And talk through touch. It is a powerful communicator. Holding hands and hugging immediately let a child know that you love him. The unique bond and energy between you floats outward. It eliminates distance. Try a daily ritual with your child: look in their eyes, squeeze their hand, and say "Have I told you today how much I love you?"

TALK OFTEN AND ABOUT EVERYTHING!

26

Spiritual Hugs and "Lub" Trademarks

When my second son, James, was five, he frequently said to me, "You're a whole bunch of roses, Mommy." Or, on another day, he would say, "You're a whole bunch of stars and flowers!" When you least expect it, children can throw you these special hugs.

"I love you—thanks for a great day!" says Thomas, lying in his bed ready to go to sleep. "I love you—thanks for a great day!" I say back to him. Then, our words quickly repeat themselves. He says again, "I love you—thanks for a great day!" And I reply, "I love you—thanks for a great day!" After several times more, over and over, we laugh or smile. I leave his room, exhausted with joy, still hearing him down the hallway saying, "I love you—thanks for a great day!" Sometimes I will yell it back again or simply smile to myself. The day has ended. We are rejoicing. We are rejoicing in each other and in our relationship. We are giving each other a spiritual hug.

Ever try a spiritual hug? It's easy. Just reach out to your children. Share a simple ritual that comes naturally to you both. There are parts to a child's growth that can be compared to a tree. The branches, leaves, and trunk are the visible strengths. They are those unique characteristics that answer the question "Who am I?" But it's the unseen roots that give valuable stability and nourishment to the tree. Nourishing spiritual roots is just as important as becoming aware of your outer strengths. Each child has spiritual roots that need to be watered and strengthened. Spiritual hugs can nourish these roots.

As time moves forward, Thomas, now older, leaves for school saying, "I love you—thanks for a great day!" I yell it back. We repeat the lines several times and smile. Sometimes his brothers will quickly add the same wish. This verbal ritual has become our "rejoice" chant. Several years later, we now have added, "You're the best!" It too is repeated back and forth.

Children have a remarkable gift for expressing their joy-filled emotions. "I love you more than a brontosaurus," Thomas says to his brother James, who replies back, "I love you more than a blue whale." Another time, "I love you more than all the leaves in the universe . . . I love you more than all the stars in the sky . . . I love you more than all the universes."

At other times, their choices are a little more earthy, like "I like you more than bananas and apples"—or more free-flowing, capturing whatever they are looking at or thinking about: "I love you more than books and pencils" or "I love you more than alligators and bunny rabbits." This chant even pops up at the breakfast table. "I love you more than cereal and blueberries and bagels."

We can experience joy from children. They can be teachers. Listen to them. Have fun together. Laugh together—a lot. Try to quit worrying about getting things done, which is especially difficult to do in a culture so focused on productivity. Toss it to the wind. Kids get enough pressure at school, and they will get enough in their future work settings. So, start laughing and when everyone joins in, the laughter, the noise will be incredibly powerful. Rejoice daily in the relationship you share with each other.

When Thomas was little, he couldn't pronounce the word "love." It came out "lub" instead. This became one of his trademarks. Look for, remember, and use these unique trademarks, or ways that a child uses words to express his feelings. Not only is it fun, but it helps you absorb their "lub" in special ways. The connection between parent and child is unique, and "lub" trademarks honor this important connection. "Lub" is shared and frequently expressed through many other trademarks in our family. Thomas has a mighty hug that holds you so deeply for

that short second—it pushes a smile out. James has a special hand wave: he wiggles his right hand so it moves like a wave rolling along. I repeat this same "lub" motion back to him. John gives a hug with his arms wrapped around you and squeezes for several long seconds, then adds a deep, natural, fully open smile.

FIND SPIRITUAL HUGS AND "LUB" WITHIN
YOUR OWN FAMILY. REJOICE!

27

At the End of Your Rope

That long and rocky 12,700-foot climb up Chair Mountain deep within the Colorado Rockies took two ten-hour days. During a 140-foot-high drop, the rappel rope slipped off my shoulder. I was hanging in mid-air, with no mechanism to guide my journey from the cliff above to the ground below. A safety rope, attached around my waist and held taut by a belayer on the cliff above, offered comfort. At this dangling point I knew two things—that I couldn't fall to my death because of the belayer's safety line and that I was completely in charge of my own experience! To correct the situation, I had to secure myself on a precariously small rock ledge, putting full trust in my belayer, another nineteen-year-old student.

During any rappel, one "rappel rope" is attached to the climber and a second "safety rope" is held in place by the belayer. A belayer serves as an anchor, holding the safety line as the climber moves down. Besides securing the climber at the end of the safety rope, the belayer's very presence offers support and encouragement. With the rappel rope now off my shoulder, I knew I had to show great poise and calm, despite the intense stress. The feeling that I was totally on my own was overpowering, even though the belayer's efforts to hold me in place were keeping me stationary.

An instructor on a ledge above could only give me verbal advice. It was just several days earlier that I had learned the basics of rappelling and strategic rock climbing, but the course had been brief. I wasn't sure if my "ropes course" had prepared me for my present situation, but I had to trust myself. Trust had always been an inner challenge in the past, but now it was

an urgent, physical one. I vividly remember the feel of the narrow rock ledge where I put my hands and feet. I remember evaluating how strong it was and how long it could hold me. The ledge felt hard as my hands moved desperately along the rocks. I thought of my belayer and had to trust that he would hold me there and not let me fall. The feeling that I was completely on my own kept returning. I had to figure out what to do and then calmly execute the plan. I had to trust myself.

We weren't really sure what the purpose of Outward Bound was twenty-eight years ago. Looking back, I think it was about listening to yourself, following your instincts, and learning about trust. Everyone has an inner voice. We must train ourselves to listen to it.

Like rock climbers, children too must learn to listen inwardly and to trust themselves. A child, much like a climber, is essentially on his own. Parents are like belayers in that sometimes there isn't a whole lot to do except hold the child in place, prevent him from falling, and offer encouragement, while he learns to listen to and trust himself.

ENCOURAGE CHILDREN TO LISTEN
INWARDLY AND TO TRUST THEMSELVES.

28

Laughter and
the Humor Tool

I look at my fifteen-year-old son, John, as he kindly carries bags and bags of groceries and packages out of our car, and I say, "I love you more than a bunch of bananas!" We laugh. He's still feeling the heavy load, so I add, "I love you more than two dozen oranges." Laughter is a powerful emotion adjuster. It lightens, soothes, even dissolves difficult feelings. It feels so good once you start that it's hard to stop. What's really fun is to keep it going for extended periods of time. These "laugh-ins" can be just as emotionally powerful as hugs. Do them now, because when your children get into their teen years, they will think you're crazy if you haven't conditioned them to it.

A news report came out at the end of 1996 that said children laugh approximately four hundred times a day while adults only laugh about fifteen times. Social scientists who have studied humor want to better understand why 385 laughs vanish. For sure, most everything is humorous to young children. They don't discriminate. Our eight-year-old laughs at so much that it's easier to note the things he doesn't laugh at!

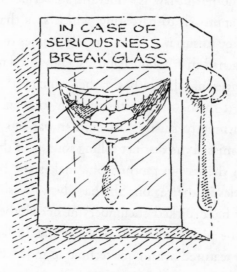

These same laugh researchers also noted the medical benefits of laughter. Giggles relieve stress, control pain, lower blood pressure, provide an aerobic workout for the diaphragm, improve the body's ability to utilize oxygen, and maximize the flow of disease-fighting proteins and cells to the blood. For health reasons, it sounds like adults need giggles more than children do. Laughter strengthens the insides, physically and emotionally. Telling jokes and doing funny things should be encouraged by everyone. The insides need these emotional releases, and it appears that daily doses of giggles are best learned from children.

My mother-in-law is a lifetime subscriber to the Erma Bombeck approach to parenting, which says that a sense of humor is key to survival. If nothing else comes to mind—just laugh. I learned that my husband, as a boy, used to frequently throw oranges into the clothes washer, which was conveniently located next to the refrigerator in their kitchen. Picture the oranges turning to slush if his mother was busy in another room and missed the distinct rolling sounds of the first cycle!

Then there's my mother. She makes the best dill and sweet pickles in the region. She has always washed the large volume of hand-picked cucumbers in her clothes washer. It shortens the pickling process dramatically. In fact, the local newspaper featured her unique technique and included photos of our washing machine when I was a teenager. Imagine how thrilled I was to show this article to my friends! When our machine had to be replaced after many years, we had to consider the availability of a "gentle wash cycle" for pickles in our next model.

There are funny stories in all families. There is humor even in those child behaviors that drive you crazy! Let me

share a few from our home front. Our oldest son, John, walks through the house and jumps up to touch the top of every door opening. This behavior coincided with his interest in basketball. If you've seen the movie *Jurassic Park*, you will recall the scene where the enormous T-Rex dinosaur is not seen yet but can be heard—THUMP, THUMP, THUMP—and felt. The earth shakes. John is T-Rex easily a dozen times a day. If I can recall the picture in my mind of the movie scene and use humor, I'm better off than if I ask him to stop jumping, which I admit I say occasionally at the *end* of the day.

When James was a baby, he frequently stood on the seat of his high chair. But he did it with such balance that it didn't bother us and, with time, we became relaxed with this "James behavior." Maybe it was even a talent. But when we went out to a restaurant, we were always reminded of his unusual "skill" when the waitress would come over and ask us to make him sit down. We replied that he was well balanced, trying to assure her that he wouldn't fall, even though he towered above us like a favorite bronze statue in our nearby park. Now, at thirteen years of age, we still catch James, chair pushed aside, standing at the dinner table. Somehow he still manages to accurately reach the growing distance from the table to his mouth with his spoon. As he has grown considerably taller, he now resembles the Statue of Liberty, as viewed from a tiny tugboat in New York harbor. He has maintained this skill, but rather than get exasperated at having to ask him to sit down, I just smile at the history here and stop acting like the worried waitress. To this day, he can gracefully stand while eating.

❈

A SENSE OF HUMOR IS ESSENTIAL—USE IT!

PART V

Creating Harmony

29

It Lasts for Always

"'Real isn't how you are made,' said the Skin Horse. 'It's a thing that happens to you. When a child loves you for a long, long time, not just to play with, but REALLY loves you, then you become Real.'

'Does it hurt?' asked the Rabbit.

'Sometimes,' said the Skin Horse, for he was always truthful. 'But when you are Real, you don't mind being hurt.'

'Does it happen all at once, like being wound up,' he asked, 'or bit by bit?'

'It doesn't happen all at once,' said the Skin Horse. 'You become. It takes a long time. That's why it doesn't often happen to people who break easily, or have sharp *edges, or who have to be carefully kept. Generally, by the time you are Real, most of your hair has been loved off, and your eyes drop out and you get loose in the joints and very shabby. But these things don't matter at all, because once you are Real, you can't be ugly, except to people who don't understand . . . but once you are Real, you can't become unreal again. It lasts for always."*

—Margery Williams, *The Velveteen Rabbit*

I know for a fact that letting a child love you enables you to become "Real." Three children have loved me for a very long time. I was thirty-nine when I had our last child. And I have become "Real." It didn't happen suddenly or quickly; it took fif-

teen years, the age of my oldest son. It wasn't painless; I went through lots of difficult learning and growth. But I didn't break. I lost my stiff, sharp edges, and I'm glad. I haven't lost my hair yet, but the gray is showing.

My joints are a little looser, but not much. My eyes haven't dropped out. In fact, I see more clearly now. And I know I'll never be ugly unless I'm with people who don't understand, because I've become "Real." But the best part, as the Skin Horse reminds me, is that I'll never become unreal again. "It lasts for always."

I want to share with you how I became real and what I discovered along the way.

❊

A CHILD'S LOVE CHANGES YOU FOREVER,
MAKES YOU "REAL," AND LASTS FOR ALWAYS.

30

The Noisy Home and Conflict

Our house is very noisy. An outsider would probably be horrified at the conflicts that play out between our walls. But I have a strong point of view about the significance of conflict and refuse to quiet all the "noise." To me, conflict is an extremely important part of all great groups, especially families. My theory goes something like this: The path to familymaking opens when children and parents freely interact with one another, and part of the natural course of any interaction is conflict. It is a normal part of group and personal relationships.

The effective parent must know how to deal with conflict in the family setting. What's the best approach? Try to resolve the conflict—right? Wrong. Let the children experience conflict. Most parents act as mediators and step in to resolve the conflict. But by doing that, they rob their children of the valuable experience of learning to deal with the conflict themselves. Conflict serves as a catalyst for the child to take total responsibility for resolving the situation. If the parent mediates, this opportunity for learning is lost.

Small families function better than large families because heightened conflict and intense disorganization is easier to resolve in smaller settings. Informality is also a key component to settling conflict because it lets conflict surface within the group. Children can practice resolving conflict by taking responsibility and making decisions. Parents can't be constantly stepping in to get rid of the conflict. They must carefully allow it to happen.

A CERTAIN AMOUNT OF CONFLICT
IS GOOD FOR CHILDREN.
DON'T BE THE INSTANT MEDIATOR.

31

The Picnic Blanket

When the weather starts getting warmer and the sun shines brighter, picnics become one of our favorite activities. Throwing some food and drinks into a basket, or even a big brown bag, and going somewhere nearby to sit in the grass is the perfect way to celebrate the arrival of sunshine and the joy it brings. Our family has a special blanket for this purpose. It's thick and soft, bumpy and beige.

The picnic blanket used to be large enough for all of us to sit on, even stretch out a little. But, as our children have gotten bigger, we seem to use every corner when it's opened up, and now fit snugly on it. Perhaps this says something about how we've grown closer together with time. We all still sit on the blanket, but it's harder and harder to share the space. So it is with living together in a group. It is not an easy thing to do, especially when children get older, larger, and more independent. They want to spread out. Sharing personal, social, and even physical space is a challenge.

Consequently, our picnic blanket is used for another purpose. Spread out on the floor *inside* the house, it becomes a forum for resolving family issues. Each member may bring up any problem or frustration to be aired "on the picnic blanket," and then we proceed to get everything out on the table (or blanket, as it were). Through discussion, a solution is reached, with the course of action decided upon by the entire group. The key to success is the willingness of all family members to approach the issue as a group problem. This not only develops mutual responsibility and respect, but it also promotes equality and total participation in decision making as well. Both are critical to the group's success, much like the sun's warmth and brightness are key for a happy picnic.

Whenever a problem seems insurmountable, the picnic blanket discussion can be used to bring the group together. Our family, for instance, needed to sit on the picnic blanket and deal with the problem of helping out with household chores. Not everyone was doing his part, and we desperately needed to figure out a solution. My husband and I felt we were doing most of the work, with very little voluntary help from our three children. Let's face it, it was no picnic for the two of us.

The solution from the picnic blanket was that each child would take total responsibility for several big chores that he liked to do and did well. John is now totally responsible for taking out all garbage, doing the dinner dishes, and cleaning the countertops. James is responsible for folding the clothes with Mom and emptying the dishwasher whenever necessary. Thomas sets the table, clears the dishes, and washes off the table after every dinner. Mom and Dad cook the meals. Mom washes the clothes, and Dad manages all the outdoor work. We each make our own bed and keep our own rooms picked up. The plan is reasonable, it has worked well, and we all feel good about it.

TRY SITTING TOGETHER ON
THE "PICNIC BLANKET" WHEN YOU WANT
TO RESOLVE FAMILY ISSUES.

32

The Worry List

When one of our sons was eleven, he worried a lot. The worries were taking over his thoughts, so we made a "worry list." I wrote down all the things that caused his worrying. He came up with nine of them.

1. **School.** "I wake up thinking WORK. I worry about whether I've done my schoolwork and what work I'm going to be doing that coming day. When I get to school it's not that bad, but sometimes I don't want to go because of the work."

2. **Home.** "My two brothers can really get on my nerves at times. I do ALL the cleaning up. They just do a little pickup, or take turns picking up toys. I'm cleaning up our fort, and they're still playing in it."

3. **Home.** "He (my brother) sings over and over again, purposefully, to drive me crazy. My other brother's scream also gets to me."
4. **School.** "I want to have a good day at school. Fun is important."
5. **Health.** "I worry that I'm going to get sick."
6. **Friends.** "I think I am losing my best friend, _____. He doesn't like me anymore. A good day is when we laugh together and sit together."
7. **Sports.** "I don't want to go out for basketball—it's too much competition, so I don't like playing it at school."

8. **Family.** "I get worried when Dad gets stressed out. This weekend, he tried to do a lot of stuff, but it seemed he did not want to do it."
9. **Brothers.** "I don't know if I am ordering my brothers around too much."

After listing each worry, we went back and discussed each one, came up with a strategy to fix it, and wrote it next to the worry. Here they are:

1. Get all homework done as soon as possible after school. Then put it aside and try not to think about it until the next day in school. Play and enjoy the rest of the evening.
2. Tell my brothers to help more with cleaning and picking up. Verbalize this each time they don't help.
3. Ask my brothers to stop singing and screaming.
4. Have fun at school, too. It's OK to be goofy and laugh.
5. Take vitamins, relax more, get more sleep, and have fun.
6. Tell my friend, "You're really a good friend of mine." Invite him over more often.
7. Don't "do" basketball.
8. Dad has to slow down! He did really want to do all that stuff, but just didn't have the energy.

9. I instinctively know when I'm too bossy and need to go with my instincts and stop when that happens.

The worry list really helped our son through his worries. Writing them down and coming up with a written plan to address them is a good activity for adults, too. It frees up our thoughts so we can live in the present.

❧

WRITING DOWN A WORRY LIST AND
THINKING UP A SOLUTION FOR EACH ITEM IS
A GREAT WAY TO REDUCE ANXIETY FOR
CHILDREN AND ADULTS ALIKE.

33

Mrs. Campbell's Fourth Grade Classroom

Families are the first and last emotional frontier. They provide fertile ground for feelings to be openly expressed and shared. Feelings are the lifeblood of a family. Parents, children, and siblings can establish a unique relationship where emotion is open and all forms of expression—sad, glad, and bad feelings—are shared. Too many parents stop the bad feelings and only want the good ones to be released. But all kinds of feelings emerge from a child's heart, and wise parents express interest in and listen to them all.

When our oldest son was in the fourth grade, Mrs. Campbell, his teacher, had the children write about their sad, glad, and bad feelings. Maybe you'd like to try a similar process with your family. Here's what our son John came up with when he did the assignment at age ten.

What I Like About Myself
I have a good sense of humor.
I am great at sports, especially swimming,
    skiing, baseball, and roller blading.
I do all my homework.
I help others with their work.
I am intelligent.
I am fair.
I laugh a lot, too much.
I love school.
I love my teacher.
I am good at getting my clothes dirty.
I love to write.
I like the environment, and I like to keep it healthy.
I am always willing to make a new friend.

It Makes Me Happy
It makes me happy when I've been gone for a long time
    visiting someone, or just gone on a vacation, and
    come back to our home, after a long plane trip.
It makes me happy when it's the start of a new season,
    spring, summer, winter, or fall. I like it because

something is always
coming—leaves,
snow, birds, and
the sun.
It makes me happy
being in school
and being with
my family.

It Makes Me Sad
It makes me sad when I
miss a lot of school.
It makes me sad when my
friend's mad at me.
It makes me sad when I
get mad at my family.

It Makes Me Angry
It makes me angry when I lose something.
It makes me angry when I get angry at someone
(like brother, friend, teacher, or parent).
It makes me angry when someone gets angry at me.
It makes me angry when someone teases me.

It makes me angry when I forget to do
   something important.
It makes me angry when I get laughed
   at (like tripping over a chair).

Feelings like these can be encouraged
within each family setting. If parents can build a
culture where emotional expression is permissible,
even contagious, then children can learn to communicate their feelings appropriately. When both
parents and children speak openly and freely from their hearts,
the family becomes a classroom for ongoing emotional learning. It is an ideal place to develop emotional expressiveness.

WELCOME AND ENCOURAGE ALL
EMOTIONS—SAD, GLAD, AND
BAD FEELINGS—THAT EMERGE
FROM YOUR CHILD'S HEART.

34

Date Night and Renewal

"Renewal" is about taking care of ourselves as people. We've discovered several ways to do this. The following rituals have helped us keep a fresh perspective and renew ourselves over the last twenty-three years.

The first is our "date night." Once a week, always the same night of the week, we have a babysitter come. We've been lucky to have the same person, Lisa, come every Thursday night for the last fifteen years. Now thirty-one years old, we've seen her grow up, too, over the years, and this has truly been our good fortune. Our children now refer to her as a "big sister." The fact that her commitment level has matched our own commitment to spend time together as a couple is not a coincidence. If "the Tao of parenting" (see Chapter 35) is activated, things often work out this way.

There are a few boundaries for "date night." It is not a time to discuss problems, financial shortfalls, or heavy-duty difficult situations, nor is it a time to compare calendars, discuss tasks, or even entertain others. "Date night" is quite simply a time set aside to have fun together. No one else is invited. It's our time to renew and care for the relationship itself. Play is a key part of this renewal. We like to take long walks together, eat dinner out, talk openly, see movies, go to rock concerts, have picnics in the park, or visit the animals in the zoo.

Another way to carve out renewal time is to make dates with yourself. Whether you are parenting alone or have a partner, time for self-renewal and nourishment is critical. Without renewal, an imbalance can occur. Your perspective on many issues will not be fresh or rich. Everyone needs space, but parents especially can get overextended. You can't nourish others unless you have been nourished first. Parents must learn to carve out some personal time for themselves, ideally every day. I've discovered that for me, there are only two possible times for this to happen—early in the morning or late at night. Sometimes, but less regularly, I'm able to sneak in some short renewal time for myself during the day, but this is quite difficult. Some of my favorite things are to: read a book, take a nap, write in my journal, garden, sit outside, slowly enjoy the newspaper, take a leisurely walk, or talk with friends. Anything that helps bring a sense of aliveness and renewal back to your personal life is appropriate.

A third way to find renewal is to take a vacation. It is essential. Going away for a short while, a two- or three-day trip, can bring sparkle back to an overtired person or an exhausted couple. The activities on this long weekend don't have to be numerous or grand. In fact, one of the best ways to restore energy is to simplify your vacation plans. Don't do much. Conserve energy, so you can release it later. Use a vacation to simplify your outer and your inner lives. Two precious days can help restore your mind and body and bring back a sense of harmony to your spirit. Take them.

MAKE REGULAR "DATES"
WITH YOURSELF
AND YOUR PARTNER.

35

The Tao of Parenting

One of our sons was losing control over his personal and social life. We didn't want him to become a control freak, but we did feel he needed to call the shots more often. If he didn't want to talk to someone at length on the telephone, he should tell them he has to go now. If he didn't want to go to a birthday party, he could say he wasn't able to make it that day. If he wasn't able to take the karate test, he should tell the instructor that he has a conflict on that date.

As we pointed these things out to our son ... BOOM ... BANG ... BRIGHT LIGHTS! ... it dawned on my husband and me that we had the same problem! *We* weren't taking enough control, and never had, of people and events in *our* lives. We would do everything asked of us and sit back and let things happen to us. So, along with our son, we all had to learn to be in the driver's seat and take hold of the controls within our own lives.

Synchronicity consists of two experiences, psychic states, or incidents, both puzzling in themselves, that occur at the same time. Importantly, their simultaneous occurrence can't be explained by pure chance. Rather, the two experiences are connected; there is a "meaningful coincidence" between them. Synchronicity means that the universe is cooperating to make something happen. Described in detail by the psychologist C. G. Jung, it suggests that events take place and people interact at precisely the right time. Occurrences appear to be arranged within the same time frame to show coincidence or coexistence. It means meeting the right people at the right time, having certain thoughts at the right moment, having opportunities open up, and even experiencing a sense of grace about the timeliness of events.

Applied to parenting, this means that the experiences of parent and child appear to be ordered by the universe. Have you experienced this ordering? I call it "the Tao of parenting." Perhaps you've noticed that your child helps you visit and revisit issues that are tough ones for you as a parent or a person. It is almost as though your child is helping you to grow and heal through the issues she brings out.

Let me share three examples of synchronicity at play from our own home front. One of our sons was keeping important issues inside, instead of getting them out and "on the table." Then we realized we were keeping thoughts inside too. He helped us see the advantage of placing our own difficult situations "on the table" so we could work through and reflect on them.

Another son conveyed to us that his confidence was low; he thought it was because he didn't have a lot of comfort when talking to people, and wanted to know how to increase his comfort level during conversations. His timing was remarkable. I had *just* experienced this same issue. I suggested that he try to live in the present while conversing with people, to simply try to enjoy the exchange itself and not worry about what others would think about him in the future. We share this personal issue now, and it is challenging us both to grow.

A final example: one of our sons wrote in his journal "At the beginning of the day I felt great. At the end of the day I felt even better." A great mood, he believes, can improve with time. This has become my personal goal now. I am trying to approach each day so it always feels "even better" at its end. It requires me to change my approach; I must conserve energy during the day so I'm not exhausted at the end. This is challenging me to change.

Children help parents visit their own needs and areas for personal growth. They can help us reflect, clarify, change, and grow, if we are aware enough to make the connections—and to see the synchronicity at play!

❀

NOTICE WHAT IS SURFACING
IN YOUR CHILDREN'S LIVES.
IT MIGHT LOOK VERY FAMILIAR.

PART VI

Culture Building

36

Emotional Glue

One day Thomas came home from first grade and said that his class had talked about "community" in school. When I asked him what it was, he said: "Community is when one person is good at something and one person is good at something else and they share it." I like Thomas's definition of community because it says that differences are good. Community means acknowledging, accepting, and sharing differences. So many parents impose their own values on their children. In the process, they teach them that they should be and think like everyone else. Families are human communities. We must learn to love one another, have disagreements, encourage differences, and still remain bonded together.

Families create powerful ties. They have an emotional glue that comes from a strong sense of interdependence. Parents and children are glued together by common identity, purpose, experiences, and culture. If a strong sense of community exists, there is a deep, fulfilling sense of belonging. The parent who lets a new value or norm become integrated into the family gives a positive sense of personal power to a child. Children can actually see the impact of their own value contributions on the family culture, and they learn it is OK to be different!

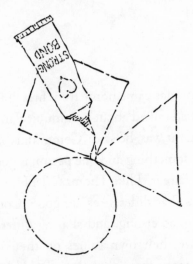

First and foremost, parents must learn to make these differences fruitful. That there is "fruit" in difference is difficult for some to accept. Most people prefer agreement, but what if disagreement were an acceptable norm? What if family differences were viewed positively? The larger task for parents and teachers is to create a context that allows and embraces genuine disagreement. Parents generally have a difficult time accepting and encouraging differences. It's hard work. It involves listening to your children, treating them as friends, and letting engaging, even disagreeing, conversation become a priority. When such conversation is encouraged within the family, parents and children can become friends and grow closer together.

LET DIFFERENCES WITHIN THE FAMILY
FLOURISH.

37

Blank Canvas

Several summers ago, we started a new family tradition—the creation of a group art project. We trek off to the local art store together and purchase a large blank canvas and lots of acrylic paints and brushes. Then we divide the canvas into six sections with a light pencil mark. This gives each of us our boundaries to work within. Since there are five of us, the sixth space is usually shared by two who want to have another smaller shared space. We all then paint our own space, taking as long as we want. The entire project is normally completed within a day, with each person usually working in isolation of the others. Anything is acceptable.

Not only is this art project fun to do every year, but we all look at it frequently and are now able to compare the years.

We can remember how old each of us was and the important things that happened. But the value of this group art project is that it is something done by our family as a group. It reminds us that familymaking is fun. It also makes everyone feel attached, connected, and part of our family. When family members complete their individual canvas spaces, an amazingly integrated painting emerges.

Everyone needs to know and feel that they belong and play an important role in the family. They need to be involved in shaping the family culture in which they live and grow. Cultural traditions, like the shared canvas, are rituals. Rituals act like glue that holds the family together. Families can develop their own rituals. Any event the family enjoys and does regularly can be a ritual. It might be a fancy Friday dinner, a walk together early every Saturday morning, or a regular walk up the local mountain. Another of our rituals is to take a daylong bike trip along Lake Michigan every summer. The best part is that there are no rules on how to define rituals. They just have to make you and your family feel special.

Rituals often begin with parents, but children's values and ideas should also be reflected in their selection. If a child wants to introduce a new ritual, parents should allow it, knowing that this will make the child feel special. Each member of the family can establish rituals and weave them into the fabric of the group.

❋

ANY EVENT THAT FEELS SPECIAL TO YOUR
FAMILY CAN BE A RITUAL AND SERVE TO
BRING THE GROUP CLOSER TOGETHER.

38

Family Culture from the Ground Up

Let's take a look at our vegetable garden again. Our family has never written down how we go about preparing the soil, selecting the vegetables, or planting and caring for our crops and harvest. Yet we each have this detailed knowledge within us. We know it without thinking or talking. It is part of our family culture.

Our culture is the shared information that tells us how to act (norms) and what is important (values). We know, for example, that everyone must play a part in selecting the vegetables. One of our norms says that the trip to the nursery cannot be missed. We also value experimentation; if one person wants to select a new type of lettuce or kohlrabi, we are open to trying these new plants, but we must have some of our

regulars too. Another norm says we need to walk on the stepping stones within the garden, and yet another, that it is very
important for each of us to take a trowel in hand, dig the holes,
and plant. Being the "total farmer" has become so important
that if one of us misses out on any task, it is upsetting.

A group's culture tells its members what they need to
know so that others within the group will accept them and
their actions. This specific "cultural information" is developed
and learned within the group. It enables members to "read"
the behavior and events that they observe, and to relate to
others in the group. When parents and children don't carry

the same "cultural information," watch out. One can see the conflict coming around the corner. It's sort of like the sudden arrival of a rabbit in the middle of our vegetable garden. There will be a confrontation. Culture must be shared from the ground up.

It takes time to learn a family's culture. No script is given to the actors. If a friend is visiting on the weekend in May when we put in the garden, we show them how we do it (our norms) and what is important (our values). A family's culture is powerful and pervasive and extremely subtle, too. Family members share their expectations, usually implicitly, about how to behave in relation to each other. They also share their norms and values through their dialogue and actions. Family members are rewarded when they accept the norms and values and feel left out when they do not.

Families, like individual countries, form unique cultures. While culture can be consciously created, too often it develops unconsciously, without concerted effort or focused vision for what its members want the culture to become. Forming a culture involves developing and sharing a common set of:

+ beliefs (values)
+ norms (behavior guidelines)
+ attitudes (points of view)
+ goals (plans for the future)
+ information (detailed cultural knowledge)

That's why family culture, like a carefully designed and planted vegetable garden, needs to be consciously cultivated by every family member in order to produce a bountiful harvest together.

CULTURE IS THE SHARED KNOWLEDGE
THAT FAMILY MEMBERS CARRY AROUND
IN THEIR HEADS AND HEARTS.
FORM YOURS THOUGHTFULLY.

39

Mirroring

Mirroring is the process of becoming part of a culture by practicing the group's norms again and again until they become automatic and habitual behavior. It enables the culture of the group to be perpetuated over time. In order for this to occur, family members watch carefully and listen intently to the spoken and unspoken signals that family members use to interact with each other. Once they have observed the "rituals" of the group, they begin to mirror, or imitate, the behaviors they have observed until they become second nature. In this way, they learn and adapt to their particular family cultures, with all of their uniqueness, peculiarities, and eccentricities.

Unfortunately, most parents want their children to simply mirror the existing family culture rather than to participate

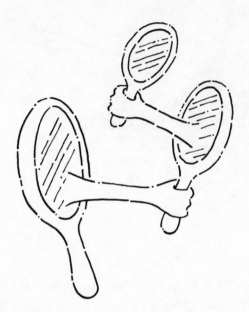

in transforming it. They want them merely to observe and imitate rather than to filter, enrich, and interact with the cultural information they receive. Sadly, under this scenario, the sparkling insights and perspectives of children don't have a chance to develop and add to the family culture—and children learn the habit of mindlessly adopting the current cultural norms. In such a family setting, you'll often hear questions from a child like "Why is it done that way?" or "Why don't you include me in that decision?" or "Why do people always argue with what the child suggests?" The typical response is: "Because that's just the way we do it around here."

I know of an authoritarian family where the children learned that no one should ever say anything "negative" at meals. Meals became show-off times where family members reported only positive news—how many As had been received at school or how many points scored in soccer. The more positive information formally presented, the better. At this family's table, there were no opportunities to express doubts, brainstorm, try out new ideas, or express more than a very narrow range of emotions.

Sharing a mistake and what was learned from it would not fit into this family culture. Such expressive behavior was considered inappropriate. The children had to learn this cultural norm in order to be accepted into that culture. They were encouraged to mirror this norm and not change their culture. Yet a child's natural way of expressing creative ideas, doubts, and thoughts can often regenerate the family culture or help it to evolve in a positive way.

Why shouldn't children have a say in the norms and values of their family culture? If we close ourselves off to our children's input because they're "just children," we disempower them with the belief that trying to change a group's culture is usually a fruitless endeavor. The culture of a family should include the desired norms and values of *all* its members. If you think this is way above the heads of children, ask some ten-year-olds what their values are. You'll be pleasantly surprised by their insights.

EVERY FAMILY MEMBER SHOULD HAVE
A SAY IN ESTABLISHING AND CHANGING
FAMILY NORMS AND VALUES.

40

Adding to the Family's Culture Pot

Every Christmas Eve my family makes clam chowder. It has become a permanent part of our holiday traditions. An observer of our kitchen scene might be surprised at our industrious and methodical activity. The five of us participate equally in preparing and cooking our chowder. We have a huge pot for this purpose. The very sight of it primes our taste buds for our scrumptious and savory stew. Together, we cut and blanch the bacon, chop and sauté the celery and onions, and dice the potatoes. Everything is added to the pot. Tomatoes are optional, and strong feelings surface every year as to whether or not we put them in. Other essential ingredients include: chicken soup stock, canned minced clams, and hot milk, which we thicken with a roux mixture of flour and butter. We also add ground black pepper, thyme leaves, and garnish with parsley.

We all know what's in our chowder. Any one of us could make it without the cherished recipe. Yet, to be sure, with five "chefs" assiduously involved, our chowder never tastes quite the same from year to year. Once the flour-and-butter roux mixture wasn't added to the hot milk at the right time, and it curdled. Another year, we tossed out the clam juice instead of adding it to the pot! And another year we undercooked the potatoes, discovering that they weren't tender nor mushy enough for our taste. (Next year, I'd like to try the recipe using fresh clams.) We've learned, however, that if we add all the different ingredients, the flavors blend together, and it tastes incredibly sensational, very rich, and healthy too.

Family culture also needs a good-sized pot. There must be room for each child's unique and personal ideas and contributions. Listen to some of our sons' contributions: Let's have a warm breakfast twice during the weekday mornings. Let's picnic or eat dinner outside once a week during the spring and summer months. Let's take one night during the week and do something totally different after school, like go see an early movie (and bring tons of popcorn), or visit the barn in the local zoo to see the farm animals that we liked when we were little, or play our favorite board games. For sure, if children are involved in "cooking" their family culture, then heartier, healthier, and more vibrant relationships simmer for everyone to enjoy.

Like our annual clam chowder, know that your family culture will be an ever-changing, always transforming creation—especially if you have lots of chefs! Decide on the ingredients together. Mix them up. Experiment. Don't forget to pour in large measures of essential ingredients like joy, love, respect, and creativity. Toss in a lot of humor too. These will always make for hearty family relationships. Warm it up, and enjoy. A rich family culture can serve its members for a lifetime.

LET EVERY FAMILY MEMBER ADD TO AND
STIR THE FAMILY'S CULTURE POT.

41

The Leader or the Pack?

W hen parents nurture the value of equality, each family member feels important because it's true! Each has equal significance within the group. This does not assume that all members have the same skills or equal gifts. There are major differences among each individual's strengths, but each person in the family has unique talents that contribute to the group, and each one can learn a lot from the others.

The strongest families are like democratic communities. Unfortunately, most families are not democratic, but patriarchal and hierarchical, and tend not to treat their members as equals. The father and mother are the authoritative figures or bosses, and the children are viewed as unequal participants in the group. These autocratic families have parents who say, "What I say goes." Rudolf Dreikurs, M.D., in his book *Children:*

The Challenge identifies characteristics for both types of families, autocratic and democratic. Where does yours fit in? The parent of a democratic family is a sensitive leader who guides, encourages, stimulates, influences, and listens. The parent of an autocratic family is an authority figure who dominates, coerces, pressures, uses power, and gives commands.

Autocratic families do not foster equality. Children in these families quickly learn that they do not have an equal part in building their family's values. Democratic families, on the other hand, have a strong sense of cooperation and community about them. Parents recommend that action be taken when it is necessary for the good of the group. There is no authority figure who stresses "You do it because I said so." Instead, the democratic parent listens to and respects each family member, encourages independence, and offers guidance in a spirit of cooperation. Children know they can contribute their individual values to their family culture and that they will be heard. Rather than punishment, there are logical consequences that teach. In this way, children are allowed to experience the consequences of their actions through real world learning situations.

Parents in democratic families are leaders, says Dreikurs:

> A good leader inspires and stimulates his followers into action that suits the situation. So it must be with parents. Our children need our guidance. They will accept it if they know we respect them as equal human beings with equal rights to decide what they will do.... We can create an atmosphere of mutual self-respect and consideration and provide an opportunity for the child to learn how to live comfortably and happily with others. We need to arrange learning situations without showing a lack of respect for the child or for ourselves.

In a democratic family, parents are both democratic leaders and wise teachers, nurturing both equality and learning.

EVERY MEMBER WITHIN A FAMILY IS 100
PERCENT EQUAL TO THE OTHERS.

42

Families Last for Always

Learning to parent is not a simple connect-the-dot activity. You don't begin at dot A, then move to dot B, and proceed through to dot Z. Nor is there one single, surefire truth about parenting. But one thing is certain—it involves your whole life. Challenges can come in any order, even several at once. An approach may work at some times but not at others. Or it may work with one child but not another. Every child is different, and there just isn't some neat technique or approach that works for them all. For sure, the familymaking process is eventful, and at times complex and arduous, yet hugely significant and rewarding.

Parenting lasts a whole lifetime. Take it slowly. The challenge is to let each child be heard, even when they all talk at once. Accept things as they are. Trust yourself. Say "yes" to the challenges that come, because "no" prevents you and your child from growing. The goal is to let parenting teach us about life, and life teach us about parenting. Try to be open to the lessons and close to the child. Staying close is the hard part, but you learn to parent by doing it. It's an all-consuming job that exposes your entire life and the beauty of who you really are. Embrace it!

Several years ago, when James was eleven years old, he wrote a poem for me on Mother's Day. It read:

Thanks for all the love,
Love, from your passionate heart,
Happiness; wonder.
Love is a balloon,
Swells up like a huge bubble,
Overwhelmed; thankful.

I love you,
You love me,
Just us two,
We're filled with glee.

Happiness is right here,
Far much closer than near,

Thanks for all your love,
Lets keep it as close as a hand to a glove!

To become "as close as a hand to a glove," place time and energy inside your family. Try to get rid of stress. It's not good for relationships. It destroys the gentleness that is required for a relationship to flourish. It gets in the way of feeling "filled with glee."

As parents, you can learn how to deepen the special relationships in your family—creating, growing, and enriching these connections until they become a potent source of energy in each of your lives. Feeling energy from the bond you share is as nourishing and necessary to the spirit as food is to the body, and remarkably, you have the opportunity to build this energy with the very persons you live and interact with every day.

I encourage you to create vibrant, alive, and rich relationships. Ultimately, the family bond is based on the art of togetherness—connecting and becoming closer, yet still remaining free to grow individually. I believe, dear friend, that the family is the most important "structure" that we have in our world. Like the pyramids of long ago, families can be sturdy, sustaining, and enduring. They can last for always.

About the Author

Dr. Susan Smith Kuczmarski is an educator who teaches teachers, a cultural anthropologist who studies family culture, a sociologist who views families as small interactive groups, and a parent who has experienced familymaking first-hand. She has done extensive research directly related to how children learn to become members of social groups and how adolescents become leaders.

Dr. Kuczmarski holds a Doctorate in Education from Columbia University in New York City, where she was named an International Fellow. Over the last twenty years, she has conducted lectures, workshops, and seminars on leadership and familymaking. In addition, she has been interviewed about leadership on radio and television, holds two additional master's degrees in sociology and education from Columbia University, has been listed in *Who's Who in the World* for the past ten years, and was recently selected for inclusion in *One Thousand Leaders of World Influence*.

Dr. Kuczmarski has taught at seven universities, worked in three nonprofit educational organizations, including the United Nations, and co-founded an innovation consulting firm, Kuczmarski & Associates, in Chicago. She is the co-author of *Values-Based Leadership*, published by Prentice Hall in 1995. She lives in Chicago with her husband, soul mate, and partner in familymaking, Tom. They continue to marvel at and learn from their three sons, John, James, and Thomas.

To obtain information about workshops and speeches available by Dr. Susan Kuczmarski:

Write to the author:
1165 North Clark Street
Suite #700
Chicago, IL 60610

Call in your request:
(312) 988-1507

Fax your request:
(312) 988-9393